Nothing More
Comforting

Nothing More Comforting

To Georgina —

Canada's Heritage Food

Dorothy Duncan

Dorothy Duncan

THE DUNDURN GROUP
TORONTO · OXFORD

Copy-Editor: Andrea Pruss
Design: Jennifer Scott
Illustrations: Catriona Wight
Printer: Transcontinental

National Library of Canada Cataloguing in Publication Data

Duncan, Dorothy
    Nothing more comforting : Canada's heritage food / Dorothy Duncan.

ISBN 1-55002-447-7

1. Food habits — Canada — History. 2. Cookery — Canada — History. 3. Cookery, Canadian. I. Title.

TX360.C3D85 2003   641.3'00971   C2003-901075-9

1   2   3   4   5   07   06   05   04   03

THE CANADA COUNCIL | LE CONSEIL DES ARTS
FOR THE ARTS | DU CANADA
SINCE 1957 | DEPUIS 1957

ONTARIO ARTS COUNCIL
CONSEIL DES ARTS DE L'ONTARIO

We acknowledge the support of the **Canada Council for the Arts** and the **Ontario Arts Council** for our publishing program. We also acknowledge the financial support of the **Government of Canada** through the **Book Publishing Industry Development Program** and **The Association for the Export of Canadian Books**, and the **Government of Ontario** through the **Ontario Book Publishers Tax Credit** program, and the **Ontario Media Development Corporation's Ontario Book Initiative.**

Printed and bound in Canada.♻
Printed on recycled paper.
www.dundurn.com

Dundurn Press	Dundurn Press	Dundurn Press
8 Market Street	73 Lime Walk	2250 Military Road
Suite 200	Headington, Oxford,	Tonawanda NY
Toronto, Ontario, Canada	England	U.S.A. 14150
M5E 1M6	OX3 7AD	

For
Carol and Barbara
with love and gratitude.

Table of Contents

Preface

Canada's culinary history is a long and interesting one, beginning centuries ago with the traditions and foodways of the First Nations. For those newcomers from Great Britain, France, and Europe who began arriving in the seventeenth century, survival was of paramount importance. The recipes, ingredients, and memories of their homelands had to be set aside as they hunted, fished, and foraged for food. From those humble beginnings an incredibly complex culinary heritage has evolved, shaped by Canada's diverse geographical regions, its fluctuating climate, and the many cultural groups that have settled here. In addition, legends, beliefs, and folklore have been part of our culinary heritage since the beginning.

Although I grew up in an agricultural community, it was not until I became the curator of Black Creek Pioneer Village in Ontario that my interest was aroused regarding the food and beverage traditions of our ancestors. Researching and interpreting Canadian foodways for public programmes became an important and fascinating part of my work. Later, as a museums advisor for the province of Ontario, I had the opportunity to work with many museum curators to research and introduce their communities' culinary history to the public through exhibits, displays, lectures, seminars, workshops, and conferences.

Nothing More Comforting

In 1982, when my good friends Joan and Donald Rumgay of Port Hope, Ontario encouraged me to start writing about Canada's food traditions, I began to realize and appreciate the enormity of the topic. As I developed this manuscript I appreciated the advice and assistance of Colin Agnew, Kerry Breeze, Jeanne Hughes, Andrea Pruss, and Barbara Truax.

Nothing More Comforting: Canada's Heritage Food is just an introduction to our long tradition of food, fellowship, and sharing in Canada. I hope this book will encourage readers to explore their own culinary heritage and to share it with family, friends, and neighbours.

Dorothy Duncan,
May 2003

Maple Magic

*The rising of the sap is felt in the forest trees; frosty nights and sunny days
call forth the activity of the settlers in the woods; sugar making is now at
hand, and all is bustle and life in the shanty.*
Catharine Parr Traill, *The Canadian Settler's Guide*

With the words "Sap's running!" one of Canada's
oldest industries gets ready to swing into action
and thousands of winter-weary Canadians prepare to celebrate the coming of spring. For centuries, the
annual tapping of maple trees (*acer saccharum*) has brought a
joyful end to winter while providing both a sweetener and
a flavouring, as well as an opportunity to enjoy good food,
good fun, and good fellowship.

Long before European contact, the First Nations living in
what is today eastern and central Canada and the northeastern
United States would watch for the "sugar moon" to appear, for
that was the signal that the magic sap was running and that
they should gather in camps near the groves of trees to harvest
it. It was a very special time for the First Nations, for it proved
that the Creator was again providing for their needs. They
would celebrate with feasting, thanksgiving, and the telling of
stories and legends surrounding this ritual. As part of their festivals, the First Nations would also pass around ceremonial

11

containers of syrup so that everyone could sample it and be strengthened by this energy-building medicine. They then feasted on favourite foods flavoured with maple syrup, such as soups, puddings, fish, fowl, and game. Quantities of the thick syrup would be poured into cooling troughs and kneaded by hand or with a paddle until it was thick and creamy. This soft sugar was poured into moulds and stored, to be eaten as a sweet or used as a flavouring during the coming year.

When the first settlers arrived in North America they were quick to copy the First Nations' methods of tapping the trees with simple slits in the bark, an inserted reed, and a hand-carved wooden container to catch the sap. Although syrups can be made from red and silver maple and from butternut and black walnut, sugar and black maples have continued to be the favourites.

Elizabeth Simcoe, the wife of John Graves Simcoe, the first lieutenant-governor of Upper Canada, describes in her diary in March of 1794 the process already adopted by the farmers:

Wed, 19th — This is the month for making maple sugar; a hot sun and frosty nights cause the sap to flow most. Slits are cut in the bark of the trees, and wooden troughs set under the tree, into which the sap — a clear, sweet water — runs. It is collected from a number of trees, and boiled in large kettles till it becomes a hard consistence. Moderate boiling will make powder sugar, but when boiled long it forms very hard cakes, which are better ... In a month's time, when the best sap is exhausted, an inferior kind runs, of which vinegar is made. Cutting the trees does not kill them, for the same trees bear it for many years following. Dr. Nooth [Superintendent General Dr. M. Nooth was on the staff of the Quebec hospital at that time and was a friend to the Simcoes], at Quebec showed me some maple sugar which he had refined, and it became as white as West India sugar. The sap of birch trees will make vinegar.

In Canada today we assume that maple syrup production is limited to an area called the Maple Belt, which includes Ontario, Quebec, and part of the Maritimes. Sugar maples are now rare west of the Ontario border; however, Jonathan Carver describes a very different situation in *Travels Through the Interior Parts of North America in the Years 1766, 1767, 1768* when he came upon Lake Winnipeg:

Lake Winnpeck, or as the French write it, Lac Ouinipoque, has on the north-east some mountains, and on the east many barren plains. The maple or sugar tree grows here in great plenty, and there is likewise gathered an amazing quantity of rice, which proves that grain will flourish in these northern climates as well as in warmer.

New arrivals were quick to copy the aspects of celebration as well, for French Canadians soon organized their own festivals for sugaring off at the sugar shanties or sugar shacks in the bush. Originally, a *Festival de la Cabane à Sucre* would have included only close family members and friends, and it would have been a very personal celebration. A great treat for the children (and young adults) at the sugaring off would be a taffy pull. Some of the syrup was set aside and usually taken into the kitchen to be boiled to a heavier consistency. Long lines of the thick syrup were dropped on pans of clean snow, and the young people were encouraged to twist the taffy around a spoon, fork, or stick in swirls and savour it slowly like a sucker.

The maple sugar harvest was not without its problems, as at least one newcomer, Samuel Strickland, described in *Twenty-seven Years in Canada West or The Experiences of an Early Settler* in 1853, when he found his cattle had enjoyed the contents of the sap barrel too much and had become very bloated, and only by puncturing the walls of their stomachs were they saved from death.

Sugar and imported flavourings were both scarce and expensive in the pioneer communities in Canada, so the availability of this sweetener and the subtle and unique taste that resulted from adding maple to foods were highly regarded. The traditional methods of making maple syrup and maple sugar remained virtually unchanged for nearly three hundred years in North America, until the middle of the twentieth century, when the modernization of techniques and the introduction of precision instruments, plastic tubing, and central evaporator plants replaced the old skills and equipment.

Unfortunately, over the years, many sugar bush owners tried to circumvent the long and tedious steps involved in the harvest and refinement of the sap, and they began to look for ways to avoid the tapping, collecting, evaporating, and filtering process. As sap is about 97 percent water, it takes about 40 gallons to produce 1 gallon of syrup, so the combination of a labour-intensive industry and the costs of shipping the syrup to markets across Canada made this a very expensive product. Cheap, adulterated imitations began to appear, often composed of cane sugar and glucose seasoned with strongly flavoured, low-grade maple sugar or extracts of coal tar.

To stop these products, The Pure Maple Syrup Co-operative and Agricultural Association was organized in 1913. The goal of the Association was to assist the members to improve and market their products — and to educate the public. Sugar bush owners soon realized that an important part of public education was to open their properties (both bush and sugar shack) to the public. In the beginning, people were simply allowed to wander around, see how much was involved in this long, slow process that is compacted into a very short time (mid-March to mid-April), and hopefully buy gallons of syrup before they left. It wasn't long, however, before the industry began to realize how fascinating this glimpse of the process was to the general public, including teachers and school classes, visitors from other parts of the continent or abroad, where sugar maples do not grow, and special interest groups. They saw the potential to educate in a broader sense, and perhaps even turn a profit at the same time.

Many sugar bush owners thus developed a complete package visit — a ride into the bush on a sleigh pulled by horses or a tractor, a tour of the operation using both pioneer methods and the latest technology, tastes of sap and finished syrup, and then, in many cases, a chance to take part in an old-fashioned celebration. Included in the last might be a table spread with an array of food: ham basted with maple syrup, baked beans sweetened with maple syrup, maple tarts, and maple sugar pie, all containing those important ingredients, maple syrup or sugar. There might be the opportunity to drop the thick syrup into the fresh snow so that it hardens and becomes a delectable morsel. Sometimes, the afternoon or evening celebration ended in dancing.

Many artifacts, such as hand-carved moulds, spiles, sap buckets, and cast iron pots, survive as mute witnesses to this Canadian tradition, an institution as well as a food source. In addition, almost every Canadian cookery book in every Canadian kitchen contains recipes using the sweet sap of the maple.

Catharine Parr Traill suggested this treat in *The Canadian Settler's Guide* in 1855:

Maple Sugar Sweeties
When sugaring off, take a little of the thickest syrup into a saucer, stir in a very little fine flour, and a small bit of butter, and flavour with essence of lemon, peppermint or ginger, as you like best; when cold cut into little bricks about an inch in length. This makes a cheap treat for the little ones.

Maple Tarts
2 eggs
1 cup brown sugar
1 cup maple syrup
3 tablespoons melted butter
1 cup raisins or currants (soaked in boiling water
and well drained)

Mix ingredients well and fill pastry-lined tart tins
about two-thirds full with the mixture. Bake at
350°F for about 20 minutes.

Maple sugar pie is a favourite with French Canadians
everywhere. Here is a very basic recipe for it:

Maple Sugar Pie
1 1/4 cups maple sugar
3/4 cup cream
2 well-beaten eggs
1 tablespoon butter
pastry for a 9-inch single crust pie

Cook all four ingredients in a double boiler until
thick. Cool. Pour into the single, unbaked crust.
Bake at 350°F for about 10 minutes, lower the temperature to 325°F and continue to bake for about
50 minutes. Cool and serve.

Signs of Spring

You needn't tell me that a man who doesn't love oysters and asparagus and good wines has got a soul, or a stomach either. He's simply got the instinct for being unhappy.
"Saki," pen name of Scottish writer Hector Hugh Munro

If we in modern Canada welcome spring with open arms, consider the emotions of our ancestors when those first signs appeared — whether in the sky, the streams, the forests, or the fields. Earlier generations of Canadians were longing not only for fresh food but also for plants that could be used as remedies to restore them to good health and to replenish their depleted medicine cupboards. Whether First Nations or newcomers, they had endured an endless winter of dried or frozen foods that had somehow survived in storage, but many of them were well aware of the deaths among their neighbours and friends in late winter and early spring from diseases now known to have been caused by vitamin deficiencies. How welcome were those first tiny, green shoots of rhubarb (pie plant to our ancestors), asparagus, fiddle-heads, dandelions, and other edible plants that today we consider weeds, as well as the early herbs that braved the melting snow.

Signs of Spring

From region to region, that special something that is a harbinger of spring often varies widely. In Eastern Canada, one of the most important signs is the fiddlehead, as the tiny, curled frond of the Ostrich Fern is commonly called. Fiddleheads grow in many parts of eastern Canada as well as in Quebec and Ontario in early spring after the annual freshets have subsided, and they have now become a favourite with gourmets around the world.

When the first Europeans arrived in Canada, the Maliseet (Malecite) First Nations were living in the river valleys of southern New Brunswick and southern Quebec. These natives utilized every aspect of their environment to improve their way of life, including using local wild plants for food, medicines, and dyes. They not only harvested and ate the Ostrich Ferns that they called *mahsos*, but they also painted pictures of them on their birch bark canoes and wigwams, showing the high regard that they had for this plant as a medicine and as a food. The natives taught the newcomers how to hunt for this delicacy along the riverbanks after the floods had subsided in early spring. There were, and still are, among the natives of New Brunswick, many legends about them, and if you are very quiet while you search, you can actually hear the ferns growing as they push aside twigs, branches, and dried leaves to emerge from the damp earth.

For the United Empire Loyalists arriving in Eastern Canada over two centuries ago and desperately searching for food in an alien land, fiddleheads provided a means of survival. Peter Fisher, writing in *Sketches of New Brunswick* in 1825, captures that desperate search for food:

The men caught fish and hunted moose when they
could. In the spring we made maple sugar. We ate
fiddleheads, grapes and even the leaves of trees to
allay the pangs of hunger. On one occasion some
poisonous weeds were eaten along with the fiddleheads; one or two died, and Dr. Earle had all he
could do to save my life.

Fiddleheads need only a little trim, a rinse in cold water,
and a short sauté in butter to be ready for the table. The
search for fiddleheads still goes on to satisfy a growing
Canadian and international demand, and as the plant has not
been successfully cultivated in other countries, it remains a
North American celebrity.

In western Canada many wild plants, such as Lambs
Quarters (pigweed) and the dandelion, are eagerly sought,
just as they have been for generations. In the days of settlement the perennial roots of dandelion would be dug up,
even in winter, to extract the juice for a patient, to be fol-
lowed by a steady diet of the tiny young leaves of the plant
as soon as they appeared in the snow. Both the roots and the
leaves can be used in salad.

Dandelion Salad
Dig up the very young dandelion plants before
they bloom. Wash the leaves and white crown
well. Soak in cold, salted water until ready to use.
Cut up and toss with wild onions and two or
three slices of well-fried bacon cut into small

pieces. A simple dressing of equal amounts of vinegar and the bacon fat warmed together can be used. Sprinkle with salt and pepper. The leaves of young plantain and clover may be substituted or included in this salad.

The newly grown roots of the dandelion are also tender and can be peeled with a sharp knife or potato peeler. They can be sliced crosswise and boiled in two waters (with baking soda added to the first water). Drain, and season with salt, pepper, and butter. Dandelion roots are also an excellent substitute for coffee, but that is another story.

Another of the surest signs of spring is the appearance of fresh asparagus. Prized by epicures since Roman times, asparagus takes its name from the Greek word *asparagus*. The name first appeared in English about 1000 A.D. A member of the lily family, there are more than one hundred different species, including the African asparagus ferns that are grown as ornamental plants. It also appears in different colours; however, the most popular is the well-known green vegetable with the succulent stalks. Eagerly awaited each spring in the local markets, it is recognized as a diuretic and one of Nature's remedies after a long, hard winter.

It is not known how asparagus reached the New World, although given its popularity in Great Britain and Europe, it was a natural stowaway on the sailing vessels crossing the Atlantic. It appears in many cookbooks of the eighteenth century in "economical" recipes, usually in combination with other ingredients. A representative example is in *The*

Complete Housewife or Accomplish'd Gentlewoman's Companion, written by Elizabeth Smith in 1727.

Asparagus Soop
Take twelve pound of lean beef, cut in slices, then put in a quarter of a pound of butter in a stew pan over the fire, and put your beef in.

Let it boil up quick till it begins to brown, then put in a pint of brown ale, and a gallon of water, and cover it close. Let it stew gently for an hour and a half. Put in what spice you like in the stewing and strain off the liquor, and scum off all the fat.

Then put in some vermicelli, some sallery, washed and cut small, half a hundred of Asparagus cut small, and palates boiled tender and cut. Put all these in and let them boil gently till tender. Just as 'tis going up, fry a handful of spinage in butter and throw in a French roll.

Asparagus appears to have continued a favourite with the well-to-do in the nineteenth century, for printed cookbooks contained recipes for it in soups, garnishes, and purées, on toast, and in combination with other ingredients. In fact, *The Home Cook Book*, compiled by Ladies of Toronto and Chief Cities and Towns in Canada and first published in 1877 in Toronto to benefit the Hospital for Sick Children, contains a recipe that is hauntingly familiar to its British counterpart 150 years before, although the portions are smaller:

Asparagus Soup

Three or four pounds of veal cut fine, a little salt pork, two or three bunches of asparagus and three quarts of water. Boil one-half of the asparagus with the meat, leaving the rest in water until about twenty minutes before serving; then add the rest of the asparagus and boil just before serving; add one pint of milk; thicken with a little flour and season. The soup should boil about three hours before adding the last half of the asparagus.

We are fortunate that, in many parts of Canada, we can enjoy some spring delights all year long. There is nothing that can really match their perfection when fresh. Look for them in the wild or in your market, general store, or roadside stand and enjoy these centuries-old treats that herald the arrival of spring.

Preserve the Pie Plant

[Medicinal rhubarb was] produced in the Province of Tangut in large quantities ... merchants who come to buy it, convey it to all the world.
    Marco Polo

Rhubarb was first described as a medicine in a Chinese herbal remedy dating from 2700 B.C., and for centuries it continued to be grown for its curative qualities. It was nurtured by the monks in the monasteries of Asia and Europe during the Middle Ages (also as a medicine), but it was not until 1777 that it was first recorded in Britain, in an herbal garden at Banbury, Oxfordshire.

In the nineteenth century some interest was taken in using rhubarb for culinary purposes, and it slowly began to appear in London vegetable and fruit markets. In 1855 the term "rhubarb pie" appeared in print for the first time, heralding a dessert that became so popular that rhubarb became known as "pie plant" in North America. Its popularity continued to grow in the nineteenth century, largely because it was so easy to cultivate.

Sometimes only a matter of days would elapse from the moment the huge leaves began to push through the melting snow in early spring until it appeared on the table. For our winter-weary ancestors without our resources of transport, freezers, and methods of preservation, pie plant was welcome for its purgative and astringent properties, as well as its tart flavour.

The American Agriculturist, published in New York in 1862, says it all:

A Spring Tart
Does anybody doubt, or not know, the desirableness of the rhubarb vegetable! Then we pity him. It is one of the finest things in the world, to make a pie or spring tart.

Apples often give out in April and May, and those which remain are wilted and tasteless. Man's stomach longs for something fresh, crisp and juicy: the pie plant affords that very thing. It forms a connecting link in the year-long chain of articles for pie making.

Think, too, of the doctor's testimony that it is "one of the most wholesome, cooling and delicious substances that can be used for the table. For dysentery in children, it is an infallible remedy, stewed, seasoned with sugar and eaten in any quantity with bread." We have tasted samples of fair wine made from this plant. It is also used for jellies and jams.

As *The American Agriculturist* points out, rhubarb wine was a popular and inexpensive beverage in the nineteenth century, and the cookery books of the period contained many basic recipes for making it. Although not so common today, the elders in many a family still remember it fondly:

Rhubarb Wine
Take 4 pounds of rhubarb to 1 gallon of water, squeeze it, put it into a tub, and pour the water on it; let it steep 3 days, then strain off the liquid; put 3 1/2 pounds of sugar to every gallon, and put it into a barrel, stir it every day for a fortnight, then add a few raisins and a small quantity of isinglass [gelatin], then bung it up for three months. Finally bottle it and in 5 to 6 weeks it will be ready for use.

Although rhubarb is a vegetable, it usually appears on our tables, just as it did on those of our ancestors, in the guise of a fruit. Like many fruits, it is most often dressed up as a dessert. From coast to coast, similar recipes have evolved in Canadian kitchens over the years to the point that any regional or provincial peculiarities have disappeared. Here are just a few:

Rhubarb Fool
1 pound fresh rhubarb, trimmed
4 ounces sugar
finely grated rind and juice of 1 orange
1/2 pint whipping cream

Cut the rhubarb into 1-inch lengths and place in a saucepan with the sugar, orange rind, and juice and bring to a boil with a little water (not more than 1/4 pint) and gently simmer until tender. Purée in a blender or food processor and place in the refrigerator until cold. Whip the cream and fold into the purée. Place in individual serving glasses and put back into the refrigerator until ready to serve.

Serve with fingers of sponge cake. Serves four.

Rhubarb-Strawberry Dessert
2 cups fresh rhubarb (cut fine)
2 cups fresh strawberries (cut fine)
1 cup sugar
2 tablespoons flour

Sprinkle a few drops of lemon juice on the mixture and then prepare the following topping:
1 cup brown sugar
2/3 cup butter or margarine
1/2 cup flour

Mix topping well and spread (it will be crumbly) on fruit. Bake in moderate oven, 350°F, for about 40 minutes. Serve warm with whipped cream if desired.

Rhubarb Pie
Make enough pastry for a two-crust pie and line pie plate. Combine 2 tablespoons sugar with 2 tablespoons flour and spread on pastry in bottom of pie plate. Fill with rhubarb that has been washed, wiped dry, and cut

into pieces. In a small bowl, combine one well-beaten egg and one cup of sugar. Pour this mixture over the rhubarb. Put on pastry top and bake in hot oven, 425°F, for 10 minutes, then reduce oven to 350°F and bake until golden brown (approximately 35 minutes).

Serve hot or cold.

Rhubarb Conserve
14 cups rhubarb (cut in 1/2-inch pieces)
3 cups raisins
7 cups sugar
juice of 2 oranges
rind of 2 oranges, thickly sliced
1/2 to 1 cup walnuts (if desired)

Combine all ingredients, except walnuts, and let stand one hour. Bring to a boil (uncovered) for 40 minutes, stirring frequently. Add walnuts and boil 5 more minutes. Put in sterilized jars and seal.

Rhubarb Marmalade
4 cups rhubarb (cut fine)
2 cups white sugar
1 cup chopped walnuts

Boil rhubarb and sugar until thickened. *Do not add water.* Add nuts and stir well. Place in sterilized jars and, when cold, seal with paraffin. Store in cool place.

Canned Rhubarb
8 cups rhubarb (cut fine)
5 cups sugar
1 cup water

Let stand overnight. In the morning bring to a boil and add 1 can of crushed pineapple or pineapple tidbits. Sterilize jars, fill, seal, and store in a cool place.

Rhubarb Relish for Meat
12 cups rhubarb
6 cups brown sugar
3 cups chopped onions
1 1/4 cups white vinegar
1 teaspoon cinnamon
1 teaspoon ground cloves
1/2 teaspoon pepper

Cut rhubarb into small pieces, wash, and dry. Add sugar and let stand for 2 to 3 hours. Add the rest of the ingredients and boil until thick (about 30 to 40 minutes). Stir often to prevent sticking. Store in sterilized jars until ready to use. Serve with meat. This is a particular favourite in Newfoundland.

Whether you are looking for a refreshing dish for the table or a spring tonic and mood brightener, turn to your rhubarb patch. Canadians, for a very long time, have been depending on this plant to cure what ails them.

Herbs of Grace

Those herbs which perfume the air most delightfully, not passed by as the rest, but, being trodden upon and crushed, are three; that is, burnet, wild thyme and watermints. Therefore, you are to set whole alleys of them, to have the pleasure when you walk or tread.
Sir Francis Bacon

In recent years, herbs have enjoyed such a surge in popularity that they have become one of the hottest items in Canadian cuisine. Gone forever is the image of herbs being used simply as inexpensive substitutes for spices or other imported ingredients. Today, herbs are considered staples by both everyday cooks and award-winning chefs. They are the subject of scores of new books, a major topic at workshops, seminars, and conferences, and the foundation for enterprising new businesses that serve this growing interest with a variety of herb-related products. In addition, organizations such as the International Herb Association and the Canadian Herb Society serve a growing membership.

With this return to popularity herbs have come full circle. They appear on the baked clay tablets of ancient Egypt and also on the wall and ceiling paintings of their tombs. The Romans left us the first written recipes using herbs both on the walls of their kitchens and in the collections of recipes of some of their famous cooks. We learn that:

> The main Roman meal was eaten in the evening and comprised three courses. The first course was made up of morsels to tempt the appetite — oysters, cheese, olives, vegetables, and that great delicacy, roasted dormice. The second course included all kinds of meat; poultry and game such as song birds, ostriches, flamingoes, sausages, and a variety of stews, all highly seasoned with herbs and spices. This repast would be concluded with a dessert of fruit.

When the Romans arrived in Britain they brought with them, as well as their own recipes, a great deal of inherited knowledge from ancient Greece, Babylon, and Egypt about the use of herbs in cooking, in medicines, and for scent and cosmetics. This knowledge filtered through the layers of society to the lowliest peasant, who would cultivate an herb garden at the door.

During the Saxon period, much of this knowledge was lost, and we find that the cultivation and use of herbs often focused on the supernatural and the warding off of evil spirits rather than their healing effects and uses as flavourings. *The Leech Book of Bald*, written about 950 A.D., details many of the superstitions and pagan rites and beliefs about the evil or the good influence of plants at that time. For example, it was commonly believed that witches inhabited the elder; the periwinkle was called the sorcerer's violet and could be used to foil the powers of evil; leeks were grown on the roofs of houses as a safeguard against lightning striking the building, or any other bad luck. Rue became known as the "herb of grace" because it enabled the eater to see witches and so avoid them, while the roots of the mandrake were believed to grow in human form and would shriek when they were uprooted. It was also believed they only grew under a gallows. Because the roots were much valued as a narcotic to ease pain and promote sleep, the legends say that a dog would be tied to the plant to pull it up so that the evil would possess the dog rather than the digger!

In the Middle Ages it was from the monasteries and the monks, who were able to read the ancient Latin writings about herbs and plants and exchange them across Europe and Britain, that herbs gained popularity as healing plants. The monks, with their dedication to the sick and the poor, frequently had large herb gardens within the monastery walls and often became the physicians for their surrounding districts.

In the manor houses of the Middle Ages, the lady of the house often developed an herb garden and a stillroom where the plants could be dried and made into medicines for her family, their servants, and any neighbours or friends who needed her assistance. In larger towns, an apothecary often opened a shop to sell herbal remedies, for only the very wealthy could afford to have a doctor in attendance, and then with questionable results!

Herbs were grown for other reasons besides seasoning and medicines, and one of the most important was to attract bees, thus leading to a source of honey, a valued sweetener. Lemon balm was often grown near the beehives, for it was believed bees would never leave a garden in which it was grown. Herbs such as lavender, fennel, costmary, cowslips, and daisies were grown to strew on the floors and perfume the room. Pomanders were made of sponge, moss, and fruit combined with herbs and were carried by doctors and monks visiting the sick and dying. In the past, herbs were also used for cosmetics, for dyes, for warding off insects, and as a substitute for soap.

Whether you grow your own herbs in windowsill pots or an outdoor garden or buy them as needed from markets or stores, there are several that are very popular and easy to use. These include such a stalwart as mint, chosen by the International Herb Association as Herb of the Year for 1998. The First Nations would gather a form of wild mint from stream banks to make an excellent beverage. They also ground the leaves and stems and dissolved them in water to treat nausea. Apple mint and peppermint are favourites for teas, while spearmint cuttings were brought by newcomers to use as restoratives and medicines, and today all three excel as cooking herbs when added to peas, carrots, potatoes, or roast lamb, or for making accompaniments such as mint sauce.

Parsley has long been the most widely used herb for flavouring, colouring, and garnishing food. The fresh sprigs of curly green leaves can be trusted not to wilt quickly, and when chopped they add both flavour and colour to a wide range of dishes.

Chives can be snipped with scissors for garnishing a dish or for flavouring when regular onions are too strong. They are ideal for salads, cold soups, omelettes, sauces, cheese dishes, and some vegetable recipes. The purple flowers can be separated into florets and added to salads for colour and flavour. Chives, like many other herbs, can also be added to soft butter to produce herb butter for bread, rolls, toast, and biscuits. Herb vinegars are easy to make as well and bring subtle new flavours to tried and true recipes.

Rosemary is a fragrant herb with a host of uses. Dumplings, biscuits, preserves, stuffings, vegetable dishes, and meats such as ham and pork all benefit from its excellent flavour. Oregano, meanwhile, is a hardy perennial whose leaves, either dried or fresh, have a strong flavour ideal for seasoning rice, pasta, pizza, and beef dishes. Oregano is often used in Italian, Spanish, and Mexican cooking.

Caraway seeds have a strong aniseed or licorice flavour and are an excellent addition to both savoury and sweet recipes. They were traditionally used by European settlers in rye breads, cakes, soups, stews, and almost any recipe involving cabbage. The next time you make coleslaw, toss in a teaspoon of caraway for a flavourful treat.

When spring arrives, why not experiment with herbs? Add them to your favourite recipes; take a workshop; read a book; exchange ideas with friends and family. Join the growing trend to learn about these mystical plants that for centuries have brought culinary magic to the kitchen.

Parsley Potatoes
1 pound potatoes
1 teaspoon salt
2 tablespoons butter or chive butter

fresh-ground pepper
3 tablespoons chopped fresh parsley
1 tablespoon chopped chives, shallots, or tiny fresh
green onions
milk or cream to cover

Peel potatoes and boil with salt until just cooked. Drain. Melt the butter in a flameproof or ovenproof casserole and slice potatoes in layers, seasoning each layer with pepper, finely chopped parsley, and chives, shallots, or onions. Heat about 1 cup of milk or cream and pour over potatoes to cover. If using a flameproof casserole, heat for about 10 minutes on a gentle heat; if in an ovenproof casserole, about 15 minutes at 350°F. Serve hot from the casserole as an excellent companion to chicken or fish.

Herb Butter
1/2 cup soft, salted butter
1/3 cup parsley, mint, or chives or
3 or 4 finely chopped or pressed garlic cloves or
1/4 cup sage, thyme, or basil

Use finely chopped, fresh, green herbs for flavouring herb butter and beat well into the softened, salted butter. You may want to sharpen it with a few drops of lemon juice. Herb butters can be kept refrigerated in well-covered containers until ready to use.

Herb Vinegar
Sterilize some small jars and wash chosen herbs —
mint, tarragon, marjoram, chives, or parsley are all
good candidates. Remove dead or bruised leaves
and dry thoroughly (or the vinegar may be
cloudy). Fill jars with the herb. Bring sufficient
vinegar (wine, cider, or malt) to a boil and pour
hot over herbs. Cork or cover well and let stand
for 2 weeks in a sunny spot, shaking or turning
upside down daily. Remove the herbs and put 1
new leaf or small bunch in each jar. Store for a
month in a cool spot and then use as needed. For
garlic vinegar, use 4 cloves of peeled garlic, each
cut in 2 for each quart of vinegar, and proceed as
described for other herbs.

Mint Sauce
6 tablespoons cider vinegar or mint vinegar
1 1/2 cups water
1/2 cup dried mint
2 tablespoons lemon juice
4 tablespoons sugar
1/2 teaspoon salt

Simmer vinegar, water, and mint for 5 minutes. Add
the rest of the ingredients and just bring to a boil
before removing from heat. Store in small, covered
bottles in the refrigerator. Serve hot or cold. If fresh
mint is used, increase to 1 cup minced leaves — after

simmering, strain through a fine sieve before adding remaining ingredients.

Roasted Vegetables with Rosemary
4 potatoes, peeled and quartered or sliced
3 sweet potatoes, peeled and cut into 1–inch pieces
1/2 small turnip, peeled and cut into 1/2–inch pieces
3 carrots, peeled and cut into 1–inch pieces
1/2 cauliflower, cut into large flowerets
10 Brussels sprouts

Dressing:
1/4 cup olive oil
1 teaspoon dried, crushed rosemary
1/2 teaspoon salt
1/4 teaspoon pepper
2 tablespoons lemon juice

Place vegetables in a large, shallow, greased baking dish. Mix ingredients for dressing and drizzle over vegetables. Place dish on a baking pan or cookie sheet, cover with lid or foil, and bake at 450°F for 30 minutes. Remove from oven and stir. Leave cover off and continue roasting for about 20 minutes until tender and brown. Serves 6 to 8. The vegetables listed above are only suggestions — any combination of these with cooking onions, green beans, broccoli, parsnips, or whatever else you have on hand can be used with equal success.

Caraway Cabbage
6 tablespoons unsalted butter
2 pounds cabbage, quartered, cored, and cut into
1/4-inch to 1/2-inch strips
1 tablespoon caraway seeds
1 tablespoon white vinegar or herb vinegar

Melt butter in a large, heavy saucepan. When foam subsides, add cabbage, caraway seeds, and salt to taste. Stir well so that the cabbage is covered with butter. Cover and let cook for about 3 or 4 minutes until cabbage is just wilted. Serve in a heated dish with vinegar sprinkled over. Serves 8.

Savoury
Seasonings

In this island there are many spices ... their Highnesses may see that I shall give them all the gold they require, spices also and cotton, mastic and aloes. I think also I have found rhubarb and cinnamon.
Christopher Columbus

Canadians seldom stop to speculate about the seasonings they add to their food, for we are so conditioned by habit, tradition, or availability that we do it automatically. With a full spice rack in the kitchen and an herb garden at the door (or sometimes in flowerpots on the windowsill) there are endless possibilities for flavouring the dishes that we prepare.

In our modern homes we often use the terms herbs and spices interchangeably when actually they refer to quite different ingredients. An herb is defined as a seed-producing annual, biennial, or herbaceous perennial that does not develop woody tissue, dies down at the end of a growing season, and is valued for its medicinal, savoury, or aromatic qualities. Spices are usually the seeds or the bark of trees or plants originating in tropical climates and have a much stronger and more pungent odour and flavour than herbs. Many herbs can be grown in Canada, while spices cannot survive in our climate and must be imported.

Nothing More Comforting

There are no records to tell us when the first person experimented with a seed or a plant and tried adding it to a joint of meat or a bowl of food or simply tried munching on it to soothe an ailment (perhaps having watched an animal do the same thing to cure a problem). Delving into the past only confirms that people have been using both herbs and spices for centuries for seasoning and flavouring food and for their aromatic and medicinal qualities in everyday life.

Legend tells us that it was the fourteenth-century writings of Marco Polo, the Venetian traveller, trader, and author of *The Book of Marco Polo*, that gave Europeans a first-hand account of the wealth of spices to be found in the Far East. Attempts to find and profit from the spices Polo described led to some of the great voyages of discovery in the fifteenth and sixteenth centuries. Pepper, first domesticated in India, was one of the first trade items between Europe and the Far East, and like many of its counterparts at that time it was widely used for medicine as well as for seasoning and preserving food. Nutmegs, from a tree native to the Molucca Islands in the East Indian Archipelago, were highly prized for their seeds, which when pulverized produced the spice nutmeg, while a second spice, called mace, was produced from the seed's covering.

As more and more spices reached markets in the Western world, cooks and housewives realized their range and scope and the fact that a little spice "would go a long way," while herbs often had to be used in quantity to have the desired effect. However, spices remained the favourites of the rich; because of their scarcity and expense, they were, for the most part, beyond the financial grasp of the middle class or the peasants. *The Family Dictionary; or, Household Companion* by Dr. William Salmon, 1695, gives us one of the medical recipes using spices:

Usquebaugh

To make this the right *Irish* way, who were the first Inventors that we can hear of: Take two gallons of rectified Spirit*, half a pound of Spanish Licorice, a quarter pound of raisins of the Sun, three ounces of Dates sliced, the Tops of Thyme and Balm, of each a pugil**; the Tops or Flowers of Rosemary two ounces, Cinnamon and Mace well bruised, of each an ounce; Annis-seed & Corriander-seeds bruised likewise, of each two ounces; Citron, or Lemon, and Orange-peel finely scraped, of each half an ounce: Let these infuse in a warm place forty eight hours, with often shaking together, and somewhat, if it may be, increasing the heat; then let them stand in a cool place for the space of a Week, sweeten it with Sugar Candy, and so draw off the Liquor, and press out the Liquid part that remains in the Ingredients. For a weaker sort, put other Spirits to them, and do as before.

This is not only pleasant to drink, but moderately taken greatly preserves the Lungs against cold Distilations of Rheums, and other Defects that afflict them, and incline them to Consumption. It lengthens the Breath, cheers the Heart, and keeps out ill Airs occasioned by Damps and Fog, &c.

41

*   Rectified spirit: a pure distilled alcohol, for which
an inexpensive vodka could be substituted.

**   Pugil: a pinch

Early explorers from Great Britain and Europe, like Vasco
da Gama, Columbus, Cabot, Magellan, and others, risked their
lives and fortunes by sailing west in search of a new route to the
pepper-, cinnamon-, clove-, and nutmeg-rich Indies, and in so
doing found instead the Americas, where the First Nations had
been cultivating something the new arrivals called peppers *(cap-
sicums)* for centuries. Those new peppers, along with beans,
corn, squash, potatoes, and tomatoes, were taken back to the
Old World as curiosities and soon transformed their cuisine.

In addition to the search for easy access there were
attempts to monopolize spices so that they would maintain
their allure, as described by William Rhind in *A History of
the Vegetable Kingdom,* 1842:

> The nutmeg is a native of the Moluccas, and
> after the possession of these islands by the Dutch,
> was, like the clove, jealously made an object of strict
> monopoly. Actuated by this narrow-minded policy,
> the Dutch endeavoured to extirpate the nutmeg-
> tree from all the islands except Banda; but it is said
> that the wood-pigeon has often been the uninten-
> tional means of thwarting this monopolizing spirit,
> by conveying and dropping the fruit beyond these
> limits; thus disseminated, the plant has been always
> more widely diffused than the clove.

The East India Company had opened up trade with those faraway lands where spices were grown, and in time, it became easier and cheaper to purchase the once elusive and exotic spices and introduce them into the recipes for puddings, dumplings, and flummery (a favourite food in Britain and Ireland for centuries, it was a sweet pudding seasoned with spices).

The first explorers, traders, trappers, and settlers reaching North America would have brought with them the knowledge of how to use both herbs and spices and of the strengths and weaknesses of both.

Mrs. Clarke's Cookery Book Comprising a Collection of About Fourteen Hundred Practical, Useful and Unique Receipts Including "Sick Room Cookery" and a Number of Excellent Receipts Entitled "The Doctor" also What to Name the Baby is typical of the Canadian cookery books of the nineteenth and twentieth centuries that included a great variety of spices and herbs in recipes. Published in 1883, the recipe for Soup Made From Bones is a case in point:

Ingredients: Bones of any freshly roasted meat, remnants of any poultry or game, fresh livers, gizzards, necks, combs of any poultry, 1 slice of lean ham, salt, 1 onion, 1 turnip, 1 leek, 1 head of celery, 4 carrots, 3 tomatoes, 1/4 of bay leaf, 3 or 4 cloves, 6 peppercorns 3 all spice, 1 bunch of parsley and chervil, tapioca, sago, vermicelli or semolina.

As the nineteenth and twentieth centuries progressed, spices became more and more available and easier and cheaper to obtain, and modern medicine gave us the "wonder drugs" of the twentieth century; with this, the use of spices and herbs as medicines almost vanished in many parts of Canada. Only in recent years have we seen a revival in their popularity and an interest in the centuries-old recipes to prevent and cure ailments of the body, mind, and spirit.

Memories live on in the minds and hearts of Canadians whenever spices are mentioned. Memorabilia live on in their homes: collectors of Canadiana rejoice in the details of the spice cabinets of the nineteenth century, those intricate little tin or wooden boxes, often gaily decorated, with tiny drawers or compartments to hold each individual whole spice. Often the cabinet contained its own grater to be used when a pinch of one spice or a dash of another was needed. How many Canadians have nostalgic memories of cinnamon toast to tempt their appetites when they had been sick in bed or as a special treat for Sunday morning breakfast? As our mothers toasted the bread, spread it with lots of butter, brown sugar, and cinnamon, and cut it into little triangles or fingers and placed it front of us, visions of those faraway places that we would never see filled our minds. Even today when we make gingerbread cookies or our Christmas puddings and cakes, the East meets the West on our kitchen counters. Herbs and spices have contributed a great deal to our Canadian food traditions and are going to continue to do so for a long time to come.

Gone to Seed

The Kingdom of Heaven is like to a grain of mustard seed ...
Holy Bible

As we reach for that little container of mustard to add to a favourite recipe or to spread on a hot dog, few of us remember this plant's historic past. There are many references to mustard in the Holy Bible, but the parable "The kingdom of heaven is like to a grain of mustard seed, which a man took, and sowed in his field, which indeed is the least of all seeds: but when it is grown it is the greatest among herbs, and becometh a tree, so that the birds of the air come and lodge in the branches thereof" is the best known, as it is mentioned by three of the apostles in the Books of Matthew, Mark, and Luke.

Mustard was well known and popular with the Greeks and Romans, not only as a flavouring and condiment for food but for its medicinal properties as well. Pliny the Elder, writing in Rome in the first century A.D., reported that:

> mustard could be used to cure hysterical swooning females affected by either lethargy or epilepsy or any person affected by a deep seated pain in any part of their body.

Nothing More Comforting

The ancients obviously tried mustard as a remedy for many ills, for by the late Middle Ages we find it described in *Herbarium*, a collection of natural remedies compiled by Franco Moria Ricci in 1980 from medieval manuscripts, as "a sure cure for gout of the big toe" *(podagra),* but it also warns that mustard affects the brain and should always be taken with almonds to avoid this side effect.

John Evelyn, a seventeenth-century Englishman, was an enthusiastic supporter of mustard as a medicine, stating, "it is of incomparable effect to quicken and revive the Spirits, strengthening the Memory, expelling heaviness, and preventing the Vertigenous Palsie." In his treatise on Sallets (salads) he insisted that it was so "necessary an ingredient to all cold and raw Salleting that it is very rarely if at all to be left out."

Settlers coming to North America from Great Britain and Europe in the late eighteenth and early nineteenth centuries brought the knowledge and skill of transforming mustard seeds into a powder that could be used to great advantage in both the kitchen and the sick room. Doctors and anxious families alike used mustard plasters to treat colds, bronchitis, pneumonia, coughing, troublesome breathing, and indeed any problem with the lungs. These plasters were a simple mixture of powdered mustard and flour mixed with water and placed between pieces of soft cloth. Sometimes the plaster was applied directly to the affected area, but more often goose grease or olive oil was rubbed on first to prevent irritating the skin. As the plaster cooled and hardened it was removed and more oil or grease applied, along with, of course, more plasters, until the patient showed signs of recovery. A hot mustard foot bath was also recommended by doctors for earache, toothache, and sinus infections.

The wonder drugs of the twentieth century have replaced the miracles of the mustard mixtures, but they live on in the memories of many Canadians who have stories to tell about the lives that were saved with these simple remedies.

The word mustard evidently comes from the French *mostarde* or *moustard* (a combination of must, a fermentation of fruit juice, and mustard seeds). Three main varieties of the plant have developed — black and white, which originated in the Middle East and around the Mediterranean and which have now spread to almost all the temperate regions of the world, and brown, or Indian, mustard, which originated in Africa. Wild mustard, or charlock, has been a troublesome weed in many parts of the world for decades, but its seeds are said to have yielded the first Durham mustard made by Mrs. Clements of Durham, England in 1729. In Britain its seeds are sometimes still mixed with those of cultivated plants to procure the desired blend. All the varieties are similar in appearance, growing from eighteen inches to four feet high, depending on the environment, and bearing tiny, spherical, hard seeds in long pods.

The many different types of prepared mustard now available on our grocers' shelves are based on a combination of the three main varieties blended with other flavourings such as wine, vinegar, spices, peppercorns, chilies, and other herbs such as tarragon and garlic. Some of the best known are:

American Mustard — a combination of white mustard seeds, white wine, sugar, and vinegar that produces a pale yellow, sweet, and mild mustard that is a great favourite on hot dogs and hamburgers.

Bordeaux Mustard — a blend of black mustard seeds, unfermented claret, and herbs that is popular with cold meats and grilled steaks.

Dijon Mustard — originated in the Burgundy area; blended from black seeds, salt, spices, and white wine, resulting in a pale yellow-grey mustard with a subtle flavour that is popular in sauces and vinaigrette dressings.

German Mustard — made from strong black mustard seeds, flour, and vinegar, it complements cold cuts and sausages.

Meaux Mustard — has an unusual crunchy texture and a hot flavour produced by a mixture of ground black seeds, spices, and vinegar, making it an excellent companion for ham and cold cuts and a welcome addition to sauces, mayonnaise, and vinaigrettes.

For our ancestors mustard was a very necessary ingredient in the pickles section of their cookery books. There were many variations of mustard sauces to preserve cucumbers, onions, and other garden vegetables for the long winter months. This recipe, taken from *The New Galt Cook Book* by Margaret Taylor and Frances McNaught, 1898, was typical:

Mustard Pickles:
One peck cucumbers, one peck onions, six heads cauliflower, one and half gallons cider vinegar, two pounds mustard, three cups brown sugar, ten cents of tumeric. Sprinkle cucumbers, onions and cauliflower each separately with salt, put on water and let

lie over night. Add the other things with a little cold vinegar, heat remainder of vinegar to boiling heat, pour over hard pickles three times, then put in all ingredients, let simmer and pour over the pickles.

Today, with our convenience foods, we can give a lift to a well-known recipe. For example, mustard butter can be made by simply adding 1 teaspoon of prepared mustard to 1/2 cup of soft butter for use on sandwiches, vegetables, fish, or meat. Mustard mayonnaise can be made by mixing 2 teaspoons of prepared mustard into a cup of mayonnaise, and an ordinary cream sauce can be transformed by having 2 teaspoons of prepared mustard added to each cup to be used on fish, seafood, meats, and vegetables. An excellent glaze for ham can be quickly prepared by combining 4 tablespoons of dark brown sugar, 2 tablespoons of liquid honey, and 1 teaspoon of mustard, applied to the ham about 40 minutes before it is finished baking.

In addition to being a quick additive to recipes, mustard is an important ingredient in many others. This is a simple one to brighten a dull day:

Baked Beans
1 pound beans soaked overnight in water
1 teaspoon baking soda
2 tablespoons vinegar
1 tablespoon dry mustard
1 tablespoon salt
1/4 teaspoon pepper

1/4 cup brown sugar
1/4 cup molasses
4 large onions, quartered
1/2 pound salt pork, cut into small cubes

Drain the beans and rinse. Cover with hot water and add baking soda. Parboil for about 20 minutes (the beans will wrinkle). Rinse with hot water. Prepare a bean pot or casserole for the oven by rubbing the sides with butter. Place some of the salt pork and two of the onions in the bottom, pour in the beans and bury the rest of the onions in them, and put the rest of the pork on top. Add the rest of the ingredients and stir. Cover. Bake 6 to 8 hours at 250°F. About halfway through the baking stage add enough boiling water to cover the beans. Keep the lid on the bean pot or the casserole until the last 30 to 40 minutes, when it should be removed so that the beans will brown. Serves about 8 hungry guests.

In Biblical times, mustard was likened to the kingdom of heaven; in modern times it is recognized as the ingredient that brings out the best in all the rest. So experiment, add a little mustard to your favourite recipe, and be prepared for some compliments.

Ginger It Up

They gave to her the nutmeg, And they gave to her the ginger; But she gave to them a far better thing, The seven gold rings off her fingers.
  The Gypsy Countess, old Scottish ballad

For centuries, spices were among the most expensive items in a household and were kept in locked compartments, cupboards, or boxes to guard against thieves. Among the most exotic and valuable, ginger was also one of the first spices known in Asia, India, and China. Among the earliest references to ginger in China is one dating to the twelfth century B.C. Confucius (551–479 B.C.) added ginger to every meal and approved its use during periods of fasting or sacrificial worship when other pungent foods were banned. It was also planted in pots and carried by the Chinese on long sea voyages to prevent scurvy.

By at least the first century A.D., ginger had reached the Mediterranean area, probably carried there by Phoenician traders. The Greeks and Romans quickly adopted this piquant, peppery spice; it was so highly prized by the latter that they paid fifteen times more per pound for ginger than they did for black pepper. The Romans were the first to use large quantities of ginger in cooking and to strew it on their floors or burn it in their homes to drive out noxious odours.

It was equally valued as a seasoning, a preservative, a perfume, and a medicine, just as it is now in many cultures. It was so well known that it was set on the table at every meal, just as salt and pepper are today, and it was a favourite seasoning for hot wine beverages called caudles. This is a modern version of one that appeared in *The Forme of Cury*, published in 1390:

Caudle
1/2 pint water
1 1/2 pints white wine
8 ounces ground almonds
1/2 teaspoon ground ginger
1 teaspoon honey
pinch salt
pinch powdered saffron

Bring the water and wine to a boil in a saucepan. Add the almonds, ginger, honey, and salt. Stir in the saffron and lift off the heat to steep for 15 minutes. Bring back to a boil and serve very hot, in small heatproof bowls.

Settlers to North America not only brought their ginger recipes with them but also found the First Nations using wild ginger as both a seasoning and a medicine. The First Nations considered the root to be an appetizer and added it to food as it was being cooked. Wild ginger was also used to treat indigestion and relieve colic and cramps.

There are many references to ginger in nineteenth-century letters, account books, and recipes, confirming the important place this spice occupied in kitchens and sick rooms. Recipes for ginger beer, wine, cookies, cakes, and gingerbread all attest to its popularity, and it was also used in cures for coughs and colds. During the twentieth century, however, ginger almost sank into obscurity among the dozens of other spices available on the shelves of general stores and supermarkets. Our parents and grandparents might have used ginger for favourite holiday recipes, but it was not often used during the rest of the year.

With more new arrivals in Canada, ginger has enjoyed an exciting revival in recent years, both in our kitchens and our medicine cabinets. With a little experimentation, ginger — ground, sliced, dried, crystallized, or preserved in syrup — can be added to many recipes with very positive effects. As well, ginger is said to be good for influenza, motion sickness, and other digestive upsets.

At one time, ginger was quite literally worth its weight in gold. That may no longer be the case, but this traditional spice is still a very valuable addition to our diet.

Ginger Pumpkin Soup
3 cups pumpkin (canned or your own, cooked and mashed)
3 cups chicken broth
1 tablespoon butter
1 tablespoon flour
3 tablespoons brown sugar
salt, pepper, ginger to taste

1 cup milk or light cream
1/2 cup finely chopped cooked ham (optional)

Combine well and bring to the boiling point, but do not boil. Serve immediately.

Ginger Salad Dressing
3 tablespoons vinegar (preferably wine vinegar)
1/3 cup olive oil
2 tablespoons brown sugar
1/4 teaspoon celery seed
ground ginger to taste
salt to taste

This is a fine dressing for any kind of spinach, lettuce, or raw vegetable salad. It is particularly good with cooked beets that have been peeled and chopped for a salad.

The following two recipes are favourites with our Canadian neighbours of Chinese ancestry, who have been making important contributions to our foodways for close to 150 years:

Beef Strips with Orange and Ginger
1 pound lean beef rump, fillet, or sirloin, cut into thin strips
finely grated rind and juice of 1 orange
1 tablespoon light soy sauce

1 teaspoon cornstarch
1 tablespoon finely chopped root ginger
2 teaspoons sesame oil
1 large carrot, cut into thin strips
2 green onions, thinly sliced

Place the beef strips in a bowl and sprinkle over them the orange rind and juice. Leave to marinate for at least 30 minutes. Drain the liquid from the meat and set aside, then mix the meat with the soy sauce, cornstarch, and ginger until well combined. Heat the oil in a wok or large frying pan and add the beef. Stir-fry for 1 minute until lightly coloured, then add the carrot and continue to stir-fry for a further 2-3 minutes. Stir in the green onions and reserved liquid, then cook, stirring, until boiling and thickened. Serve hot with rice noodles or plain boiled rice. Serves 4.

Ginger Chicken with Cashews
4 chicken breasts
1 teaspoon ground ginger
1 cup chicken broth
2 tablespoons olive oil
1 cup celery, washed and cut diagonally
1 large onion, sliced
4 ounces cashew nuts
1 teaspoon soy sauce
small dash Tabasco sauce
1 tablespoon cornstarch

Remove chicken from bones and cut into bite-sized pieces. Sprinkle with ginger and set aside. Heat the olive oil in a large frying pan (or wok) and stir-fry the chicken for about 5 minutes. Add celery and onion and continue to stir for another 3 to 4 minutes. Stir in cashew nuts, chicken broth, soy sauce, and Tabasco sauce and bring to a boil. Dissolve cornstarch in a little cold water and slowly add to the chicken mixture to thicken. Continue to boil gently for about 5 minutes and serve hot. Serves 5 to 6. This dish is good with white or wild rice.

Meanwhile, Canadians from other cultural groups were developing their own specialties using ginger as an important ingredient.

Ginger Ice Cream
4 cups milk and/or cream
2/3 cup honey
4 egg yolks
2 teaspoons cornstarch
2 teaspoons vanilla
pinch salt
1 tablespoon preserved ginger syrup
2 ounces chopped preserved ginger

Slowly bring milk to a simmer in a heavy-bottomed saucepan. Meanwhile, in a bowl, whisk together the honey, egg yolks, and cornstarch. Add half the hot milk, then pour the mixture back into the saucepan. Stir constantly over medium heat until thick enough to coat the back of a spoon. Lift off heat and stand saucepan in cold water. Stir in the vanilla, salt, ginger syrup, and chopped ginger. Freeze, preferably overnight. Stir several times to move the ice cream from the edge of your container to the middle. If you have an old-fashioned, hand-turned ice cream maker, or a modern one, this will give you even finer results. Serve with ginger wafers.

Ginger Wafers
1/4 cup molasses
1/4 cup corn syrup
1/2 cup butter
2/3 cup brown sugar
1 egg
3 cups flour
1 tablespoon ginger
1 teaspoon baking soda
1/2 teaspoon cinnamon
1/4 teaspoon ground cloves
1/4 teaspoon salt

Heat molasses, corn syrup, butter, and sugar over medium heat until ready to boil. Remove from heat and transfer to bowl or leave in saucepan if it is a large one. Let cool. Blend in lightly beaten egg and the rest of the ingredients, stirring well all the time. Cover and put in a cool place until firm enough to handle (about 2 or 3 hours). Prepare a floured surface, cut dough into quarters, and roll out as thin as possible. Cut into shapes and bake in a 375°F oven on greased baking sheets for about 8 minutes. Remove from sheets immediately. Makes about 5 dozen.

Sugar Plums
1/4 pound dried figs
1/4 pound pitted dates
1/4 pound seedless raisins
1/4 pound dried apricots
1/2 pound crystallized ginger
1/2 pound blanched almonds
1/2 pound walnut pieces
1/2 pound Brazil nuts
grated rind of 1 orange
enough lemon juice or brandy to bind the mixture
together
fruit sugar

Process or grind the dried fruits, nuts, and ginger to a coarse cut in your food processor, or chop very small with a sharp knife. Add orange peel and mix well. Add enough liquid to bind mixture together. Shape into balls and roll in fruit sugar. Store in a cool place. This is a very forgiving recipe and deletions and/or substitutions do not change its excellent flavour.

Is There a Devil in the Dairy?

Little Miss Muffet Sat on a tuffet, Eating her curds and whey; There came a big spider, Who sat down beside her, And frightened Miss Muffet away.
Sixteenth-century rhyme

About ten thousand years ago, when the first animals were domesticated, milk, butter, and cheese became an important part of our ancestors' diet. The white liquid, which in Old English was called *milc*, came from the mammary glands of cows, goats, and sheep, and it has been consumed at one time or another by most of the world's people.

Attitudes to drinking milk have changed dramatically over the centuries, and they have also depended on our station in life. In the Middle Ages, for example, the wealthy believed that milk was intended only for the elderly, invalids, and children, while the peasants all tried to keep at least one cow, which furnished their daily food — curds and whey, buttermilk, butter, and cheese.

We read about butter in the Holy Bible, usually with references to honey, indicating how special this food was to the ancients. It is believed that, like yogurt, butter was discovered accidentally by wandering herdsmen carrying milk in goatskin vessels on their camels. The jolting of the beasts acted as a sort of churn, agitating the milk, and either butter or yogurt was formed. Butter was well established as an important food in Europe and Great Britain by the Middle Ages; by the twelfth century the Germans were exporting butter to Norway, and butter made in Normandy was being sold in Paris by the fourteenth century.

Many types of vessels were used as churns, but it was not until about 1600 that a wooden churn was developed in Normandy. It appeared soon afterward in Switzerland, and it was to be the prototype for the churns that our ancestors knew so well. These churns survive today in many museum collections and in many homes as a nostalgic reminder of the past.

Despite its popularity in the Old World, milk was not known in the New World until the Spanish and the English brought milk animals. The First Nations in the Americas would have been introduced to this magic liquid by the newcomers to their shores. For the early settlers in Canada, milk was a traditional part of their diet, well known as a beverage, and an important ingredient in cooking and baking. Every settler wanted to keep at least one cow to provide a steady supply of milk and cream for use on the table, in recipes, and in creating butter and cheese. The pioneering years demanded that every housewife carefully husband her resources. Mrs. Child in *The Frugal Housewife*, published in 1832, dedicated her work to "those who are not afraid of economy." She not only taught her readers how to clean and restore their textiles and fabrics with skim milk, but also how to restore food with it:

Is There a Devil in the Dairy?

As far as it is possible, have bits of bread eaten up before they become hard. Spread those that are not eaten, and let them dry, to be pounded for puddings, or soaked for brewis. Brewis is made of crusts and dry pieces of bread, soaked a good while in hot milk, mashed up, and salted, and buttered like toast.

The temperance movement also promoted milk, as it was considered, like water, to be an appropriate beverage to be enjoyed by those who had given up the demon alcohol. The well-being and success of many Canadian farmers depended on the health of their cattle and a good yield of milk. Despite their best efforts, they often had cows go dry, sour milk, rancid butter, or bad cheese. They could not believe that these misfortunes befell them because of unhygienic conditions in their barns and dairies, and often attributed these mishaps to witches, fairies, the evil eye, or the Devil himself.

The last half of the nineteenth century brought growing concerns about the purity of milk, especially in the towns and cities of North America. Breweries often operated dairies, and the cows were sometimes fed fermented mash. In addition, milk was often stretched (adulterated) with water, chalk, and other ingredients, leading to illnesses such as "milk evil," the "trembles" or the "slows," and "milk poison."

It was Louis Pasteur, a French chemist, who demonstrated in the 1860s that abnormal fermentation of wines and beer could be prevented by heating, and he then applied the same theory to milk. Harmful (often deadly) microorganisms were destroyed by heating milk, thus rendering it a safe and wholesome food and also preventing spoilage. Pasteurization, as the process became known, was not immediately adopted in Canada, and in the late nineteenth century many Canadians, particularly children and young adults, contracted tuberculosis from the bovine type bacilli in milk. It was Adelaide Hunter Hoodless, the broken-hearted mother of a beloved son who died in 1889 from drinking impure milk, who was shocked into action by what she thought to be her own negligence. Mrs. Hoodless realized that many Canadian countrywomen did not know the importance of nutrition, hygiene, and home economics. Supported by Erland Lee, a young farmer, Mrs. Hoodless called a meeting at Squire's Hall in Stoney Creek, Ontario on February 19, 1897, to voice her concerns and to organize the countrywomen into a group. This, of course, was the founding of the Women's Institute, a movement that soon spread across Canada, to Britain, and around the world, and which is still a vital network today.

To make butter, the thrifty housewife would skim the cream from each day's milk after it came in from the barn and set it in pans in a cool place. Every day she would taste her pans of cream to decide if any were "ripe" or "on the turn." This meant, in her opinion, that the cream would be sour by the next day. She then scalded her churn and the utensils to be used — bowl, paddles, spades, and ladles — and poured the cream into the warm churn, closed the lid, and began the rhythmic movement of the dasher up and down, up and down. If there were children in the household they would be pressed into service at this point, and they would keep at the task until the butter came, often chanting:

> Come butter come,
> Johnny's waiting at the gate,
> Waiting for a butter cake,
> Come butter come!

When the churn was opened, the liquid cream had, hopefully, broken into butter and buttermilk. Using a butter paddle, the pieces of butter floating in the buttermilk were carefully lifted out into the big wooden butter bowl, leaving the buttermilk aside for baking, medicine to treat dyspepsia and fevers, or food for diabetics. It could be sealed in glass or ceramic containers with tight-fitting lids and stored for some time. The butter was then washed many times with clean, cold water until all cloudiness disappeared. If salt was to be added, and it usually was, either as a preservative or to improve the flavour, it was worked into the butter at this time. The butter was then stored in crocks in a cold place, printed into oblong or decorative moulds for use on the table, or taken to the local general store to be bartered for imported items.

There were days that, despite chanting the rhyme and hours of churning, the butter simply wouldn't come, and then the family would decide that "the devil was in the churn" and the cream would be set aside for another time when the devil had left (or perhaps the cream was finally the right age to be made into butter).

Nothing More Comforting

In Canadian homes in the nineteenth century there were no substitutes for butter, and it was an important ingredient in many recipes as well as a spread for bread, toast, tea biscuits, and scones. So for almost two hundred years butter has been a staple in most Canadian kitchens, unless religious or dietary restrictions banned it.

Our love affair with milk and its products continues — by the glass, in milk shakes, in hot chocolate, sauces, soups, scalloped potatoes, puddings, desserts, and as an additive to tea and coffee. Our babies and children thrive on it, and we consider our refrigerators empty without an ample supply on hand. These recipes containing milk and butter have been enjoyed by Canadians for decades and are still used today, a tribute to milk and butter's enduring popularity.

Shortbread
1 cup sugar
2 cups soft butter
4 1/2 cups flour
pinch of salt

Mix together the flour, sugar, and salt. Rub in the butter until you have a smooth dough. Roll or pat the dough onto a cookie sheet in a circle. Notch the edges with thumb and forefinger. Prick with a fork. Bake at 300°F for approximately 1 hour, or until pale brown in colour. While still warm, cut into wedges or strips.

Is There a Devil in the Dairy?

A Modern Syllabub
grated rind and juice of 2 lemons
1 pint whipping cream
1/2 cup sugar, or to taste
3 egg whites
1/4 cup white wine
2 tablespoons brandy

Add the rind and juice to the whipping cream and
whip until thick and stiff. Add sugar to taste. Beat
the egg whites until very stiff and fold into the
cream mixture. Gradually add the wine and brandy.
Pour into serving glasses and garnish with sprigs of
mint. Serves 10 to 12.

Scalloped Potatoes
6 potatoes
1 onion
flour
salt and pepper
milk
butter
grated cheese (if desired)

Select a baking dish and rub the interior with butter. Slice potatoes thinly and chop the onion into
small pieces. Alternate layers of potato and onion
and sprinkle each layer lightly with flour. Sprinkle
with salt and pepper and a few pieces of butter.

Cover potatoes and onions with milk, grate the cheese on top if desired, and bake 1 hour in a moderate oven of 350°F. Serve hot.

Custard Pie
3 eggs
1/2 cup white sugar
1/4 teaspoon salt
2 cups milk
grated nutmeg
pastry for one pie shell

Line pie plate with unbaked pastry, crimp edges, and set aside. In bowl, beat eggs, add sugar and salt, and finally add milk. Pour into pie shell. Sprinkle grated nutmeg on top of filling. Bake for 10 minutes at 450°F, then reduce heat to 350°F for about 20 minutes or until golden brown. Serve cold.

Bunny Borss, in the *Alberta Pictorial Cookbook*, 1988, confirms for us that:

Biscuits built the west as surely as railroads and cattle did! They provided a quick treat for visitors, they stretched the family meal, they fed hungry people who had nothing else ... and they've remained good to this day!

Is There a Devil in the Dairy?

Buttermilk Biscuits
2 cups flour
3 teaspoons baking powder
1 teaspoon salt
4 tablespoons chilled butter
1/2 teaspoon baking soda
3/4 cup buttermilk

Sift flour and baking powder together. Add salt. Cut in butter. Dissolve baking soda in the buttermilk and add slowly. Mix with a fork, turn out on a lightly floured board, pat with hand to 1/2-inch thickness. Cut with biscuit cutter. Place on cookie sheet. Bake in a hot oven, 475°F, for about 12–15 minutes. As soon as they are taken from the oven, brush all over with sweet milk. Serve hot or cold, with jam, honey, or preserves.

More Cheese, Please

Many's the long night I've dreamed of cheese — toasted, mostly.
Robert Louis Stevenson

Legend tells us that the first cheese was made accidentally by a traveller in the Middle East named Kanana, who was carrying milk in a pouch made from an animal's stomach. When he stopped to drink from his canteen he found that the contents had coagulated into a custard-like mass. When he sampled this mass he found it pleasant and nourishing and hastened to tell his friends about it.

What had happened in the sun-warmed pouch was that the rennin (an enzyme found in the lining of calves', kids', and lambs' stomachs) had transformed the milk into curds and whey — a fundamental step in the production of all cheeses.

Cheese and butter may have been made soon after the domestication of the cow, probably about 9000 B.C.; certainly cheese is mentioned in the *Vedic Hymns* of India (2,000–3,000 B.C.) and in the Old Testament of the Holy Bible.

Sailors, soldiers, and travellers for centuries have carried cheese to sustain them on their travels. It was so highly prized that it was one of the first media of exchange among Mediterranean peoples and later among European tribes.

With the rise of Christianity in Western Europe some of the finest cheeses were made by monks, from secret recipes.

In Great Britain, cheese making was originally a home industry, except on special occasions such as the birth of a child, when neighbours would join together to make a wheel of cheese. The family would be given the wheel and they would cut out small pieces to eat from the centre each day. On the day of the christening, the child was passed through the hole in the centre of the cheese for good luck.

The first settlers coming to Canada brought with them the knowledge of cheese making as a home industry and the love of cheese as an everyday item for their diet. French settlers made a soft cheese known as *fromage raffiné*, the Pennsylvania Germans made *schmier käse* and *hand käse* (ball cheese and pot cheese), while settlers from the British Isles made cheddar cheese. The United Empire Loyalists introduced the dairy industry to the area along the St. Lawrence River, the Bay of Quinte, and the Niagara Peninsula of Ontario, as well as to the Eastern Townships of Quebec. Cheese was being exported from Nova Scotia as early as 1764.

On June 4, 1864, the first small Canadian cheese factory was opened near Norwich in Oxford County, Ontario, by Harvey Farrington, who had arrived in Canada from New York State the year before. It was called "The Pioneer."

The *Hamilton Spectator* described the new factory:

It is a plain, neat looking wooden building — not costing, we should imagine, more than $1,000 complete. On the ground floor are large, double vats in which the milk is placed. These vats hold some 400 to 500 gallons of milk. The milk is delivered by the farmers twice a day in the hot weather and at the present season in the morning only. They have used during the present season the milk from 130 to 140 cows. It is paid for generally in cheese, at the rate of one pound of cheese for every ten pounds of milk, less a charge of two cents a pound for bandages, etc. At this rate, and placing the cheese at 10¢ a pound, the yield of ten average cows, we are informed would be $12.50 a week. The curing room which occupies the whole of the second story, is devoted entirely to this purpose and is arranged with very ingeniously contrived stands to facilitate the turning of the cheeses. In this room we found 200 cheeses, weighing about 80 pounds each. As for the cheese made, we can vouch for its being equal to any American cheese we have ever tasted.

Ten tons of cheese were produced the first year and shipped directly to a dealer in England.

By 1865, four more factories had opened in Oxford County, one had opened in Farmersville (Athens) in Eastern Ontario, and the Dunham Factory in Quebec that had been constructed the year before began exporting cheese. Factories were first established in New Brunswick in 1869, in Nova Scotia in 1870, in Prince Edward Island in 1882, in Manitoba and Alberta in 1886, in Saskatchewan in 1891, and in British Columbia in 1895.

The establishment of cheese factories revolutionized this home industry and transferred the labour from farm homes, where it had usually been performed by women, to the factories, where it was performed by men. Isabel Skelton in *The Backwoods Woman*, 1924, describes this commonplace activity that had provided a product that could be used for barter or trade or to supplement the family's diet:

> Cheesemaking, an industry which the modern dairymaid practically never undertakes, was a great business for my grandmother. She was mistress of the whole process. Not only did she make the cheese but she also made the rennet ... Cheesemaking, as carried on by the wives of early settlers, was a work very typical of the time.

Canada gained a great deal of publicity in the nineteenth century by making and exporting cheese "mammoths." Towards the end of the nineteenth century several large cheeses weighing between five thousand and fifty-five thousand pounds were prizewinners at international exhibitions, culminating in a Canadian cheese winning first prize at the World's Fair in Chicago in 1893, with a cheese weighing eleven tons.

You too, can follow in your grandmother's footsteps, without mishap:

Nothing More Comforting

*

To make potted cheese
1 1/2 cups grated cheddar cheese
1/2 pound soft butter
1/2 cup plus 2 tablespoons dry sherry
pinch of mace

Thoroughly combine the ingredients and press into a bowl. Cover tightly and chill. Serve with crackers or with fruit.

French Rabbit or Rare-bit
Butter an earthen dish, and place in the bottom a layer of buttered bread, then a layer of thinly cut cheese, suitable for a rabbit and alternate layers of buttered bread and cheese until the dish is full, having cheese on top. Turn over this two cups of milk into which two eggs have been beaten. Bake twenty minutes. This is less work than to make the ordinary Welsh rabbit, and it may be seasoned with beer, mustard, and Worcestershire, if desired.

Hood's Practical Cooks' Book for the Average Household, 1897.

Calcadden
This casserole is known by several names, depending on the country of origin of the cook! This is a Scottish version:

Equal amounts of potatoes and cabbage, well boiled, drained, and mashed. Butter a baking dish and mix potatoes and cabbage well. Cover with milk, salt and pepper to taste. Grate cheese liberally over the top. Bake in a medium oven for about 20 minutes. Serve hot.

Cheese Soufflé

Put two tablespoonfuls of butter in a saucepan and one heaping tablespoonful of flour; when smooth, add one teacupful of milk, one-half teaspoonful of salt, and a little cayenne pepper, and cook for two minutes; then add the well-beaten yolks of three eggs and one breakfast cupful of grated cheese, and set it to one side to cool. After it is cold, add the whites beaten to a stiff froth, turn into a buttered dish, and bake for about thirty minutes, then serve immediately.

The Cook Book by "Oscar" of the Waldorf, compiled by Oscar Tschirky, 1896.

To make a cheese ball

Thoroughly combine equal parts of cream cheese, grated cheddar cheese, and blue cheese. Mould into a ball and roll in chopped parsley or chopped nuts. Chill. Serve with crackers or fruit.

Aside from the major cheese manufacturers, there are numerous small cheese factories across Canada. The bulk are in Ontario and Quebec, but other regions have their share, too, including the Maritimes, Manitoba, Saskatchewan, Alberta, and British Columbia, and many are producing prizewinning cheese for international competitions. Many of these cheese factories are open to the public and are a must on country excursions. Be sure to visit one in your area.

Sunny Side Up

Humpty Dumpty sat on a wall, Humpty Dumpty had a great fall. All the king's horses, And all the king's men, Couldn't put Humpty together again.

Ancient nursery rhyme

From the beginning of civilization, the egg has been surrounded by legends of fertility, magic, fortune, and witchcraft. Many ancient peoples believed eggs had magical qualities of fertility — before doing their spring ploughing, farmers in Europe and Asia would smear their ploughs with a mixture of eggs, flour, and bread to ensure a good harvest. Brides in France would break an egg as they entered their new homes to promote good fortune in the years ahead. Eggs have long been a symbol of rebirth and renewal and were also considered by many to have healing properties. Most importantly, of course, eggs have for centuries been a staple in the human diet.

In North America, the eggs of quail, geese, turkeys, and pigeons were an important part of the First Nations' diet. European settlers brought chickens with them, but domesticated hens' eggs remained an expensive item until the nineteenth century. As settlements developed, every family kept a few fowl, and eggs consequently became one of the

75

standard items of barter housewives could use at the local general store to acquire much-coveted imported items. In the late nineteenth and early twentieth centuries many new egg creations were invented — scrambled in 1864, shirred (cooked in moulds) in 1883, the western sandwich and omelette, devilled eggs, Scotch eggs, eggs Sardou, and the legendary eggs Benedict. For lovers of Chinese food, it was also during this period that Egg Foo Yung was created.

Chicken coops and poultry sheds have now virtually disappeared in Canada, the egg man no longer visits us, and the poultry farm or ranch has emerged as the main supplier of fresh eggs. Unless we have allergies or cultural restrictions on their use, eggs are still a staple in Canadian kitchens because of their economy, versatility, and usefulness. Eggs are a valuable source of vitamins A, B, and D. They are low in calories and easily digested. They can be used to bind other ingredients together; to make cakes rise; to thicken sauces or dressings; to glaze foods; and to clarify liquids. There are also countless ways to cook and serve eggs as dishes in themselves: boiled, poached, fried, baked, scrambled, or cooked in omelettes or soufflés. Most egg recipes are extremely versatile and allow you to use your imagination by adding to them or by serving them with combinations of herbs, vegetables, meat, and fish.

For centuries, diviners and dreamers have used eggs to foretell the future. Now it's our turn to foretell the future of the egg. We know it's the most compact, convenient, and readily cooked little package of nutrition the world has ever known. A century ago, *Hood's Practical Cooks' Book for the Average Household* said it all:

Is there a lean sauce? an egg enriches it; a meagre cake? an egg helps it out; a barren breakfast table? an egg supplies the want; nourishment for an invalid called for? an egg does the duty. The egg is the universal resource for whatever is lacking.

It was true in 1897 and it's still true today. Enjoy!

Egg Foo Yung

Beat 4 eggs lightly and combine with 1 cup bean sprouts, 1 tablespoon chopped scallions, 1 tablespoon water chestnuts, and salt to taste. Add 3/4 cup chopped seafood or cooked meat. Mix well. In a skillet or wok with 3 teaspoons oil, drop 1/3 cup egg and vegetable mixture in small cakes and cook until browned. Pile cakes together and pour over them a sauce made from 1 cup chicken broth, 1/4 teaspoon sugar, salt, 2 tablespoons soy sauce, and 1 tablespoon cold water in which 1 teaspoon of cornstarch has been dissolved. Serve hot. Contrary to popular belief, this recipe was not developed in China, but right here in North America.

Baked Eggs

This is one of the oldest known ways of cooking eggs. They may be prepared in individual cocottes or ramekins, or several may be baked together in a small casserole dish. Put about 2 tablespoons of cream into the dish, break eggs on top, and put a small piece of butter on top of each egg. Bake in a 300°F oven.

Eggs Columbus
It is believed that Christopher Columbus brought chickens to the West Indies. This recipe, named for him, is a delicious variation of Baked Eggs.

small firm tomatoes or green peppers
salt and pepper
butter
fresh eggs
squares of toast
tomato sauce

Dip tomatoes or peppers into boiling water and slip off skins. Drain and dry. Cut each one around the stem and remove seeds. Sprinkle interiors with salt and pepper and place in a buttered small pan. Break an egg into each, season with salt and pepper or other spices, and bake in a 350°F oven about 12 minutes or until eggs are set. Lift each one carefully onto a piece of hot buttered toast. Serve with tomato sauce.

Scotch Eggs
Also called Scots Eggs, this recipe is a favourite with all Canadians, not just those of Scottish ancestry. Try them for breakfast, at a picnic, as a savoury, an *hors d'oeuvre*, or with a salad.

1 pound sausage meat (2 cups firmly packed)
5 hard-boiled eggs, with shells removed
1 large egg, well beaten
sprinkle of flour
dry white breadcrumbs
deep fat for frying

Dust each egg with a little flour. Divide the sausage meat into five portions, and on a floured surface shape each portion into an oval. Place an egg in the centre of each oval and mould sausage meat around it, making sure there are no cracks. Put beaten egg on one plate and breadcrumbs on another. Roll each egg gently in the liquid egg and then the bread-crumbs so the surface is completely covered. Heat a deep fat fryer about half full of oil to 350°F, lower in the eggs, and cook for about 5 or 6 minutes. When cooked, drain and cool. These may be cut in halves, quarters, or eighths lengthwise and served alone or as garnish on another dish.

There are several ways that we in North America serve eggs, virtually unknown in the rest of the world. Here are just a few:

Egg-in-the-Hole
Melt butter, margarine, or bacon fat in a frying pan. Butter both sides of a slice of bread and cut a circle (about 2 inches) out of the centre of the slice. Lay

bread in frying pan with the circle beside it. Break an egg into hole in bread and fry gently until it begins to cook. Flip over and cook on other side. Flip circle until it's nicely browned. Serve on a warm plate with bacon, ham, mushrooms, or vegetables, and place fried circle on top of egg and garnish with parsley.

Devilled Eggs
6 hard-boiled eggs, peeled
3 tablespoons salad dressing or mayonnaise
salt and pepper
1 teaspoon powdered mustard (optional)
1/2 teaspoon white wine vinegar (optional)
1/2 teaspoon Tabasco sauce (optional)
paprika

Cut eggs in half lengthwise and remove yolks. Set whites on a platter. If you want a zesty flavour, mix mustard, vinegar, and Tabasco sauce in a small bowl and then add other ingredients. If you want a restrained flavour, mix yolks, mayonnaise, salt, and pepper only. Mound filling into whites. Sprinkle tops with paprika. Cover and refrigerate until ready to serve.

Eggs Benedict
4 slices peameal bacon
2 English muffins
butter

4 poached eggs
3/4 cup Hollandaise sauce
cayenne pepper or paprika

In a large skillet fry bacon over medium heat until lightly browned. Drain on paper towel. Toast English muffin halves, place on each plate, and spread with butter. Top each half with slice of bacon. Prepare 4 poached eggs; lift from water with a slotted spoon, let drain, and set on top of bacon. Spoon 2 or 3 tablespoons of Hollandaise sauce over each egg. Sprinkle with light dusting of pepper or paprika and serve immediately.

Basic Hollandaise Sauce
4 egg yolks
8 ounces butter (cut into small bits)
2 tablespoons fresh lemon juice
1/8 teaspoon cayenne pepper
salt

In a double boiler over simmering water, whisk egg yolks until thick (about 1 minute). Whisk in butter, bit by bit, until it is blended and sauce begins to thicken (may take 1 to 3 minutes). Do not leave! Whisk in lemon juice and pepper until it's cooked but not curdled. This step may take only a few seconds, so be prepared to remove immediately from heat. Add salt to taste. Transfer sauce to heatproof bowl and set in a large pan of hot water until ready to serve.

Basic Soufflé

In a heavy saucepan, melt 3 tablespoons butter; add 3 tablespoons flour and 1 cup milk. Bring to boiling point and season with salt and pepper. Remove from heat, add yolks of 3 eggs, beat until thick and smooth, then slowly fold in beaten egg whites. Turn into buttered baking dish (preferably one with straight sides) and bake in a 350°F oven for 25 minutes. Take from oven directly to table and serve immediately.

The Staff of Life

A loaf of bread, the Walrus said, Is what we chiefly need:
Pepper and vinegar besides Are very good indeed—
Now if you're ready, Oysters, dear, We can begin to feed!
  Lewis Carroll, *Alice Through the Looking-Glass*

Bread has been called "the staff of life" and is one of the foods that have been with us ever since our wandering ancestors started to settle in one place to cultivate plants, ensuring the continuity of their food supply. Wheat suitable for breadmaking does not have a wild ancestor and probably evolved from the accidental crossing of two or more wild grasses. In prehistoric times wheat, barley, and millet were known to be reliable grains for cultivation, food, and storage. Egyptians, skilled as bakers and brewers, prized the wheat exported from Alexandria, which probably became the ancestor of the grain that swept into Europe and Britain. Our fondness for white bread probably began with the Greeks, who firmly believed that bread made from refined flour sifted many times was superior to any other bread and that only the wealthy classes deserved to eat it.

Bread subsequently played an important role as the centuries passed, not only as food but also as a social indicator in the hierarchy of households and communities. Britain was to eventually become famous for its "beefe, beere, and breads." Among the types of bread that made it famous was the manchet, a fine, white, soft bread that only the wealthy could afford to buy. It was often served on roundels, attractive wooden plates decorated around the edge with verses, Biblical figures, or symbols of the seasons.

A unique English bread was the cottage loaf, two round loaves baked one on top of the other. These loaves were baked on the floor of the oven and were probably designed to economize on space in a small oven.

Another unusual English bread was made from very coarse flour, and when the loaf was several days old it was made into trenchers. The slices, or cuts, of bread were then used instead of plates. When the guest was finished eating the trencher was thrown to the dogs or put in the alms baskets for the poor.

Wheat came into North America with the settlers, and when it was planted in virgin Canadian soil, it succeeded beyond anyone's wildest expectations. The new arrivals also learned from the First Nations the merits of using cornmeal for bread and baking. When settlers could not reach a gristmill to have their grain ground into flour, they improvised with hand-turned querns or pounded their harvest in a mortar and pestle. Simple, unleavened combinations of flour or meal and water that were baked over open fires, in bake pots, in brick ovens, or on griddles or girdles included bannocks, biscuits, and scones.

Leavening agents were produced in a number of ways and were usually unreliable for those pioneer housekeepers. One of the most trustworthy was baking powder, and

The Staff of Life

Catharine Parr Traill describes its virtues in *The Backwoods of Canada* in 1836:

> This powder imparts no ill taste to the bread or cakes, producing very light cakes with no trouble. Emigrants should provide an article of this kind among other sea stores as a convenient and wholesome substitute for raised bread, for the use of themselves and their little ones.

A few years later she described several other methods of making leavening agents. These included hops, yeast made of sugar yeast, brewer's yeast, barm (a combination of potatoes and hop yeast), American yeast, and a salt rising mixture. A number of carbonates such as saleratus, pearlash, carbonate of soda, and sol volatile were also mentioned in Canadian cookbooks.

Advertisements began to appear in major cities and towns for commercial bakers, such as this one in Toronto in 1856:

Loaf bread	Crackers and Mixed
Tea buns	Cakes for Tea
Short Bread	Rolls for Breakfast
Lunch Cake	Plum Cake
Wine Biscuits	Orange Peel Cake
Soda and Cabin	Abernethy Biscuits
Biscuits	Elgin Biscuits

With these new innovations and the accessibility of bakers' bread, many homemakers in eastern and central Canada gave up the mixing, kneading, and setting of dough to rise overnight (either in the dough box beside the fireplace or in a metal container on the back of the cookstove). For a few cents they could now purchase loaves, rolls, scones, and other yeast products of a standard quality. Gone was the uncertainty of ovens that were too hot or too cool, wood that was not dry, kindling that was not chopped finely enough, and the devastating effect of the weather on baking day! For the homemaker in western Canada, these were the pioneering years, and in outdoor ovens and cookstoves heated with dried buffalo chips, crusty loaves of bread were being baked from the hard spring wheat for which the Prairies became famous.

The post-war years brought to Canada waves of new immigrants from around the world. These newcomers were to have a dramatic and enduring influence on agriculture, food production, and tastes. Many immigrants came from countries where climate, soil, or culinary preferences dictated that dark breads, either black or brown, were favourites. Bakeries sprang up to serve these new international tastes, and Canadians of every culture began to experiment with, and to enjoy, breads such as pumpernickel, rye, graham, and their other dark cousins. In addition, home breadmaking has enjoyed a revival. Books, magazines, newspapers, cooking schools, and classes proclaim "Bread Baking Made Easy," and Canadians are responding to the challenge. Long discussions with grandmothers, mothers, and other relatives and friends, exchanges of forgotten recipes and cookery books, and comparisons of the best method of kneading and the merits of different brands of flour have again become popular. Why not give it a try?

If you have any hesitation about baking bread, here are some tips and some recipes that are guaranteed to produce good results and make you feel like a pioneer:

Tips for Baking Bread
- Grease bread pans with vegetable shortening.
- Bake loaves on lowest oven rack.
- Bake rolls, buns, and fancy breads on middle rack.
- Bread is finished baking when the bottom and sides of each loaf are evenly browned and when the tapped loaf sounds hollow.
- Turn bread out of pans immediately and cool on wire racks, away from drafts.

Oatmeal Bread
4 cups boiling water or milk
2 cups oatmeal
2 tablespoons lard
2/3 cup molasses
1 tablespoon salt
1 yeast cake or 1 package yeast
approximately 6 cups flour

Pour boiling water or milk over oatmeal and lard, cover, and let stand one hour. Add molasses, salt, and yeast (dissolved in warm water). Add flour slowly, beating it in with a knife. Let rise until double in bulk, knead down, shape into loaves, and let rise again. Bake at 375°F for 40 minutes.

Whole Wheat Bread
Warm 3 cups milk and pour into a large bowl with
3/4 cup brown sugar, two teaspoons salt, and one
tablespoon butter. Cool. Add 1 yeast cake or 1
package of yeast dissolved in 1/2 cup lukewarm
water that has become bubbly. Mix well and sift in
enough whole wheat stone ground flour* to make
a stiff dough. Turn out on floured board and knead
until smooth. Grease bowl, and set to rise in a warm
place. Cover bowl with cloth. When double in bulk,
turn onto a floured board and knead again. Shape
into loaves, place in pans, cover with a cloth, and set
to rise again in a warm place. When double in bulk,
bake in moderate oven, 350°F, for 35-45 minutes.

*whole wheat stone ground flour is available from
several museum villages in Canada, and from health
food stores

Steamed Brown Bread
1 cup graham flour
1 cup white flour
1 cup cornmeal
pinch salt
1/3 cup molasses
1 large teaspoon baking soda dissolved in 2 cups
plus 2 tablespoons sour milk. Mix well and steam
for 4 hours.

Tell the Bees We Need Them

The King was in his Counting House, Counting out His Money
The Queen was in the Parlour, Eating Bread and Honey
        Ancient nursery rhyme

Beekeeping, that special skill of caring for and manipulating colonies of bees, is one of the oldest forms of animal husbandry known to man. Its exact origins have been lost over the centuries, but as bees are entirely dependant on flowers for food, there is no doubt that bees and the flowers they pollinate evolved simultaneously during the earth's history. Honey is mentioned frequently in the Holy Bible; the ancient Egyptians realized its effect on other ingredients, particularly when fermentation took place; the Romans prized honey because sugar was still unknown. The Egyptians stored honey and water together so that it would turn to mead, and honey and fruit together so that it would turn to wine, both very desirable beverages. The Romans ate their main meal of the day in the evening, and one of their delicacies was made of pieces of bread dipped in milk, fried in oil, and covered with honey. When fresh fruit was out of season, preserved fruit was served, such as grapes stored in barley, or apples, figs, plums, pears, or cherries packed in honey.

During the Middle Ages, when sugar was imported into Britain from the Mediterranean area, the cost was so high that only the very wealthy could afford to buy it, and as a result honey continued to be the everyday sweetener.

The first beekeepers attempted to domesticate colonies of bees in cylinders of bark, reeds, straw, mud, earthenware, and other materials. These cylinders were modified and eventually developed into the hive-like structures that we recognize today. In Europe the standard hive was dome shaped and woven from straw. It is a symbol that has come to represent industry and thrift whenever we see it — a tribute to the bees and their habits.

Bees native to the Old World were brought to North America in the seventeenth century. In retrospect it is a miracle that a colony of bees survived the voyage across the Atlantic Ocean, given the habits and needs of the honeybee and the difficulties and length of the voyage at that time. The new environment must have been very suitable for this new arrival, for a visitor to Philadelphia in 1698 said:

Bees thrive and multiply exceedingly here. The Swedes often get great stores of them in the woods where they are free for anybody.

A visitor to New York at about the same period observed, "you will scarce see a house but the south side is begirt with hives of bees which increase after an incredible manner."

The First Nations soon came to recognize this insect as a companion of the newly arrived colonists and called it "the white man's stinging fly."

In North America the settlers made hives of hollow logs with a board nailed across the end to contain the colony they hoped to keep. These were called "bee gums." Various attempts were made with other types of hives, including the dome-shaped type woven from rye straw that survives in many Canadian museums. Eventually, a simple box about one foot square appears to have become the Canadian favourite. The great difficulty with beekeeping was, of course, the extraction of the honey, and this was usually accomplished in the fall of the year by destroying the colony and taking their harvest.

Despite its long history, beekeeping had not changed for centuries until the 1840s, when Moses Quinby of New York tried an experiment with his colony to solve the age-old problem of killing the bees to harvest the honey. He placed boxes that would hold about five pounds of honey over the hole in the top of the box hives. By replacing these boxes as they became full he developed a method of multiple-storey beekeeping so that the actual nest of the colony was not disturbed. About the same time, he invented the bellows smoker that was so useful in quieting the bees during handling.

In 1851 the Reverend Lorenzo Loraine Langstroth invented a movable frame hive that made it possible to completely inspect the inside of the hive without harm to the occupants. Within two years, both he and Quinby published books outlining the discoveries and beekeeping methods, and the foundation was laid for the modern industry that we know today.

Honey has been prized not only as a food in both the Old and New Worlds but also as a medicine and an important ingredient in the making of cosmetics and scents. In ancient Egypt the most famous of all perfumes was the sacred *Kyphi* that was burned in the temples at sunset as an offering to the setting sun. Plutarch wrote about this scent, "Its aromatic substances lull to sleep, allay anxieties, and brighten the dreams. It is made of things that delight most in the night." The ingredients that went into the making of *Kyphi* were the sweetest, heaviest spices mixed with honey and raisins steeped in red wine.

Honey was one of the earliest known humectants (a material that would hold moisture), and this made it very desirable in the making of cosmetics. Its rich, creamy consistency and the fact that it would not sour or spoil were added benefits, and as a result it was added to creams, lotions, and salves. It appeared in many recipes to prevent baldness:

> Take three spoonfuls of honey, and three handfuls of vine tendrils. Pound the tendrils well, express the juice and mix with honey. Wash the parts with it where you wish hair to grow long and thick.

A great deal of folklore has been passed on to us concerning bees and their abilities. If, for example, you want to know if it is going to rain, simply watch the bees. If indeed rain is on the way, they will not leave their hives. If there is death in the family the hives should be draped in black, a mournful tune hummed, and the name of the departed announced. As messengers to heaven they will then take the news to the Almighty.

In Canada today the industry has changed dramatically. Until very recently it was still quite common to see a few hives not too far from the kitchen dooryard in rural areas. This is becoming a rare sight as the industry moves into the hands of larger producers.

Despite the changing traditions of beekeeping, Canadians are fortunate that this natural food, so well loved since prehistoric times, is still so easily available today. At any time of the year it can be purchased at farmers' markets, health food stores, and retail stores. From July to September watch for stands at farmers' gates and at roadsides. When you are buying honey, remember that the flower will influence the colour; the paler the honey, the milder the flavour.

When we examine the cookery books of our ancestors, we find honey in combination with other ingredients concentrated in the recipes for the making of beverages and cosmetics, such as the following found in *The Everyday Cook Book* by Miss E. Neil, 1892:

Wrinkles in the Skin
White wax, one ounce; strained honey, two ounces; juice of lily-bulbs, two ounces. The foregoing melted and stirred together will remove wrinkles.

Honey was recommended as a perfect accompaniment at breakfast or at afternoon tea to be served with toast, rusks, tea biscuits, and scones. It was not until the end of the nineteenth century that we began to find recipes that featured honey in combination with other ingredients. *The Boston Cooking School Cook Book*, by Fannie Merritt Farmer, 1896, was one of the first to include recipes featuring honey:

Honey Bread
2 cups flour
1 teaspoon baking powder
1 teaspoon soda
1 teaspoon salt
1/2 teaspoon cinnamon
1 teaspoon ginger
1/2 cup strained honey
1 egg, slightly beaten
1 cup milk

Mix and sift dry ingredients. Add others. Beat thoroughly. Bake in loaf or bread stick pans in moderate oven, 350°F. Makes 1 loaf.

Very quickly other cookery books copied this trend and developed recipes of their own, or perhaps expressed in print for the first time what was actually going on in the kitchens of the nation. *The Five Roses Cook Book,* Lake of the Woods Milling Company Limited, 1915, contained several recipes using honey:

Honeycomb Gingerbread
1 1/2 pounds treacle
1 1/2 ounces ground ginger
1/2 pound sweet butter
6 ounces blanched almonds
1 pound honey
1 1/2 ounces carbonate of soda
Five Roses flour to make moderately thick dough
3/4 ounce tartaric acid

Make a pit in 5 pounds Five Roses flour, then pour in the molasses and all the other ingredients, creaming the butter. Then mix them altogether into a dough. Work it well, then put in 3/4 ounce tartaric acid. Put dough in buttered pan, and bake for two hours in a cool oven. To know when it is ready, dip a fork into it; if it comes out sticky, put in oven again. Otherwise, it is ready.

Honey Cookies
2 eggs
1 cup sugar
1 cup honey
1 teaspoon soda
1 tablespoon ginger
1 tablespoon cinnamon
Five Roses flour to roll

There are no specific directions given for baking these cookies, except for the general directions given at the beginning of the chapter:

Filling the cookie Jar:
Cookies, like pastry — because of the large proportion of fat they contain — should be thoroughly chilled before any attempt is made to roll out the dough. Roll rather thin. Use a pancake turner for lifting the cookies into the pan for baking, also in removing the cakes after baking. Cookies should bake in about 10 minutes. The oven should be rather quick, not too hot, however, as these cakes burn very easily. Cookies are at their best when two or three days old.

Today Canadian cookery books abound with recipes using honey in every conceivable combination. Add it to some of your favourite recipes and savour this ancient, mysterious sweetener that our ancestors loved.

Fairy Rings and Other Magic Morels

He that high growth on cedars did bestow
Gave also lowly mushrumps leave to grow.
  Robert Southwell, "Scorn Not the Least"

Through the centuries, mushrooms, truffles, and other edible fungi appear over and over again in the legends and folklore of people all over the world. The ancient Greeks and Romans prized them as delicacies, believing they were "the food of the gods." Because of their sudden appearance and even quicker demise, many cultures attributed to mushrooms supernatural powers — messengers of Mother Earth.

These edible fungi are found all over the world, and in some countries they were a staple, as in Tierra del Fuego, where the natives lived almost entirely on mushrooms. In Australia, some species are still called native bread.

The French were quick to realize the value of mushrooms and truffles. Because of their flavour, they gave them an important place in their cuisine, integrating them into everyday cookery more completely than any other country. The Fairy Ring mushroom, which grows in circles on lawns and pastures, but never in the woods, is still very popular in France. It retains its flavour longer when it is picked, dried, and used during the winter for soups, stews, and sauces.

In Great Britain, the great culinary passion was making mushroom ketchup (or catsup) in the eighteenth and nineteenth centuries. This relish was a valuable asset to home cooks and was used in a variety of dishes, including gravy and soups. It was also found to restore youth and flavour to fried or stewed mushrooms. These comments and recipe from *The Cook's Oracle*, written by Dr. William Kitchiner and published in 1823, give us some indication of the importance of mushroom juice at that time:

Good Catsup

If you have Good Catsup, gentle reader, make it yourself, after the following directions, and you will have a delicious Relish for Made dishes, Ragouts, Soups, Sauces or Hashes.

Look out for Mushrooms from the beginning of September. Take care they are the right sort, and *fresh gathered*. Full grown Flaps are to be preferred: put a layer of these at the bottom of a deep earthen pan, and sprinkle them with Salt, then another layer of Mushrooms, and add some more salt on them, and so on alternately, salt and mushrooms; let them remain two or three hours, by which time the salt will have penetrated the mushrooms, and rendered them easy to break; then pound them in a mortar or mash them well with your hands, let them remain for a couple of days, not longer, stirring them up, and mashing them well each day; then pour them into a stone jar, and to each quart add an ounce of whole Black Pepper; stop the jar very close, and set it in a stew-pan of boiling water, and keep it boiling for two hours at least. Take out the jar, and pour the juice clear from the settlings through a hair sieve (without squeezing the mushrooms) into a clean stewpan; let it boil very gently for half an hour; those who are for SUPERLATIVE CATSUP, will continue the boiling till the Mushroom juice is reduced to half the quantity, it may then be called Double Cat-sup or DOG-sup.

The first European settlers arriving in North America found the forest filled with hundreds of varieties of mushrooms — many more than they had known in their homeland. The First Nations used many types in their cooking. For example, the Iroquois harvested the large balloon-shaped puffballs to fry and to add to soups. Another variety, Meadow Mushrooms, one of the most common, was picked, diced, and fried, just as today.

The newcomers regarded new varieties with a healthy respect despite their urgent need for food, knowing how difficult it was (and still is) to identify edible types. Advice was given at every turn, and *The American Agriculturist* was no exception:

Mushroom Culture
Mushrooms are greatly esteemed on account of their peculiar and delicious flavour. They may be stewed, fried in fat, or made into catsup. In some countries,

Russia and Poland among the number, there are said to be above 30 kinds in use. They are there gathered at different stages of growth, and used raw, boiled, stewed, roasted, and even dried for winter use.

Great care must be exercised in selecting mushrooms for eating, as there are poisonous kinds. Three ways are recommended by which to determine whether they are good:

- by the colour of the gills, that of the good kinds being, when young, of a fine pink, or flesh colour, changing however, to that of the questionable kinds — a chocolate colour — at more mature growth;
- by the smell, the good kinds emitting an agreeable odour, while that of the bad is nauseous and disagreeable; and
- by sprinkling salt upon the inner or spongy part, unwholesome kinds turning yellow, and edible kinds black. Bad kinds are found mostly in forests; edible ones in open pastures, most frequently in old horse pastures, which sometimes, in damp, warm seasons, yield large crops.

The twentieth century has yielded cultivated mushrooms in abundance, so we are seldom tempted to walk in woods or pasture to gather wild ones. Recent discoveries have also provided a new understanding of the wildly fluctuating effects of mushrooms on people in different situations. Some are poisonous, while others are only toxic when ingested with certain foods or beverages (such as alcohol). There are mushrooms that elicit allergic responses while others impart unusual reactions. For instance, European gypsies and the First Nations of the American Southwest used some varieties for their intoxicating and hallucinogenic properties.

The twentieth century has also brought us a wealth of recipes using mushrooms, both raw and cooked. Here are a few favourites.

Tomatoes Stuffed with Mushrooms
8 ripe tomatoes
1/4 cup breadcrumbs
2 tablespoons butter
1 cup small mushrooms lightly cooked in butter and chopped
a pinch of pepper

Slice off the tops of the tomatoes and scoop out the insides and mix with breadcrumbs, butter, pepper, and chopped mushrooms. Add a pinch of salt if needed. Fill the tomatoes with the mixture and bake at 350°F for approximately 15 minutes.

This recipe is almost identical to one appearing in *Modern Cookery* by Eliza Acton in 1845. At that time, tomatoes were finally accepted as wholesome, but they were always cooked and never eaten raw.

Mushrooms au gratin
Pick, clean, trim, peel, and stem some mushrooms, place them (gills up) in a well buttered baking dish and sprinkle with white breadcrumbs, Parmesan cheese, chopped ham, and a little minced parsley and chives. Season with salt and pepper and several dabs of butter. Bake for 15 to 20 minutes at 325°F.

Fried Mushrooms
Pick, clean, trim, and peel the mushrooms. Melt some butter in a frying pan and fry mushrooms in it for about 10 minutes; season with salt and pepper. Take the mushrooms out of the pan and keep hot in the oven until ready to serve.

Mushrooms on Toast
Fry some rounds of bread cut about 1/4-inch thick and a good quantity of peeled mushrooms. Place some crispy fried bacon on the round of bread. Pile the mushrooms on the bacon and top with some parsley butter. Serve hot, and be prepared to serve seconds!

Try any of the above recipes and inject a little mushroom magic into your cooking. And while you're conjuring up your favourite mushroom dish, reminisce about the fairy tales and the little elves that once sat upon a toadstool.

Catch of the Day

The best fish that are bred in our Canadian waters are the salmon-trout, the masquinonge, white fish and black bass.
Catharine Parr Traill, *The Canadian Settler's Guide*

For centuries, the seas, lakes, and rivers of the world have been our larder. Fish and other types of seafood have provided us with not only food for our tables but also fertilizer, meal, oils, glue, and fine leather. Adopted by early Christians as the symbol of Christ, the fish has appeared in the symbolism and folklore of almost every country of the world in some form.

Primitive man probably hung fish over a fire to cook or used the earth as an oven to steam or roast them. Thousands of years later, the baked clay tablets of ancient Egypt gave us the first written recipes describing the herbs that could be used to season fish or game.

During the Middle Ages in England there were 110 fasting days in a year, including Fridays and the six weeks preceding Lent. When the Holy Church ruled that meat could not be eaten on a fast day, fish took its place. It was stressed at that time, and by subsequent writers, that this was not a papal superstition but a national obligation to support and increase the home fishing fleet, the only nursery there was for Queen Elizabeth I's navy.

Oysters began an unprecedented rise to popularity in the eighteenth century. Plentiful and very cheap, they were sold from wheelbarrows along the streets in the towns and cities of Great Britain. Large oysters were pickled, made into *ragout,* or used in stuffing. Small oysters were used in soups or stews and eaten raw. The early settlers coming to North America brought with them their love of oysters, and they continue to be popular in Canada to the present day. Many Canadian towns and villages printed handbills and advertisements announcing Oyster Suppers in local halls and churches, while in Halifax in 1866, Edward Foley of Somerset House advertised in the *Morning Chronicle*:

> Oysters and Cider. The subscriber has lately received from the country, Wallace and Annapolis, respectively, a superior lot of both of the above articles. He begs to inform the public that meals at all hours can be obtained upon reasonable terms.

There are over 350 types of edible fish in the world, so no wonder the settlers brought with them not only their love of oysters but also their knowledge of how to prepare many other types of seafood as well. Canada's maritime provinces have, since the earliest days of settlement, successfully farmed the Atlantic Ocean, the Bay of Fundy, and the St. Lawrence River and have developed some of the world's most famous seafood recipes. One of the most colourful names belongs to:

Solomon Gundy
1 salted herring
1 small onion
1 teaspoon pickling spice
vinegar

Clean the salted herring, remove the head, fins, tail and scales. Soak overnight in cold water and in the morning drain and cut the fish into pieces about 1/2-inch wide. Place in a bowl, and cover with vinegar. Slice the onion very thin and put in the vinegar and sprinkle pickling spice on top. Place in a cool place for about 24 hours, and serve with bread and butter or toast.

In Newfoundland, one of the most beloved recipes is for:

Fish and Brewis
dry salted cod
stale bread
fat salt pork
pepper

Remove the skin and large bones from the cod and soak in cold water overnight. Soak the stale bread in cold water overnight as well. In the morning, cut the salt pork into small cubes and fry until crisp. Remove from pan and set aside. Drain the water off the fish and cover with fresh cold water, bring to a boil, drain again, and bring to a boil again. Allow to simmer until fish is tender, drain, flake, and remove any bones.

Meanwhile, bring the stale bread to a boil in the water in which it was soaked. Drain, and keep warm. Combine the fish, bread mixture, and salt pork. Toss lightly in a saucepan and serve hot.

Despite the 350 edible fishes worldwide, the salmon is considered by many to be the king of fish, and for centuries, salmon has been an important staple for the First Nations. Indeed, in several Native languages the same word is used to refer to both "salmon" and "fish." The First Nations also attributed supernatural powers to the salmon, believing that their destiny and that of this superb fish are linked in eternity as in everyday life. Salmon was readily available and could be easily cooked, smoked in a wooden cage made of branches hung over a fire or planked on driftwood or alderwood to allow the embers of the fire to roast it. Modern cooks wanting to copy this traditional method can begin by heating a hardwood plank about 3 inches thick, 16 inches wide, and 3 feet long in front of an open fire or fireplace. If bricks or flat stones are available, the plank should be placed on its edge to heat. Meanwhile, clean the salmon, removing the head, tail, and fins. Sprinkle the inside with salt and close for a couple of hours while the plank heats. Place the salmon on the plank, securing it with branches or green saplings tied or nailed in place. Sprinkle the salmon with flour and stand the plank in front of the fire, allowing about 10 minutes cooking time for each inch of thickness of fish. Served with hot butter brushed overtop, this makes an incredibly simple but delicious meal.

Eric the Red was probably the first explorer who recorded seeing "larger salmon than we have ever seen before" in the north Atlantic waters in the tenth century. It was so plentiful that there are records of the first settlers on the eastern seaboard complaining about their steady, dull, and unchanging diet of salmon, and of indentured servants insisting on having a clause in their contracts limiting the frequency they could be fed salmon to once a week!

Salmon is found in both the Atlantic and Pacific Oceans as well as in the lochs, fjords, and rivers of northern Europe. The Atlantic salmon usually ranges in weight from ten to twenty pounds, although some fishermen tell of eighty-pound specimens. There are several species of Pacific salmon, including the quinnat (also known as Chinook, tyee, or king), sockeye (red or blueback), humpback (pink), coho (silver), and dog (chum). Some of these species can weigh as much as one hundred pounds. Both Atlantic and Pacific salmon have international reputations for being among the finest fish in the world and are sold as delicacies in many international markets.

As well as smoking and planking, salmon can be prepared in a variety of ways. It can be baked, poached, fried, grilled, steamed, potted, pickled, or combined with other ingredients in a range of dishes. It is best served fresh, but frozen and canned salmon retain flavour well and are convenient alternatives. The following recipes demonstrate how simple it is to prepare this royal dish, one of Canada's culinary treasures.

Baked Salmon
1 whole salmon
1 chopped onion
2 tablespoons melted butter
2 cups bread crumbs
1 teaspoon poultry seasoning or your favorite combination of herbs
1 teaspoon salt

Clean and dry the fish, leaving on head and tail, but removing the eyes. Make stuffing of bread, onion, butter, and seasoning. Sprinkle cavity of fish with salt and stuff. Tie or skewer closed. Dot salmon with butter. Wrap in foil and bake for approximately 1 hour at 350°F. Open foil to test if salmon flakes easily and finish for about 10 minutes with foil open. Garnish with lemon wedges.

Salmon Puff
2 cups flaked salmon, either fresh cooked or canned
3 cups mashed potatoes
2 egg yolks
1/2 teaspoon salt
1/4 cup minced onion
1/4 cup minced parsley
2 egg whites, beaten stiff

Mix flaked salmon, potatoes, beaten egg yolks, salt, minced onion, and minced parsley well. Fold in stiffly beaten egg whites. Pour in a buttered casserole. Bake for about 30 minutes at 350°F. Serve immediately.

So, if you can't catch your fish, or buy one that someone else has caught within the last twenty-four hours, Canadian stores offer us many canned varieties, and you can still enjoy the harvest from Canadian waters!

The Sweet Strawberry

Doubtless God could have made a better berry, but doubtless God never did.

William Butler

A s Canadians from coast to coast savour the first fresh strawberries of the season, it is difficult to grasp that this old friend is the result of mankind's spirit of adventure, and a lucky accident.

Tiny, wild, woodland strawberries had been known for centuries in Asia and Europe when two quite separate voyages of discovery brought back to the Old World samples of two new varieties from the New World. When crossed, these two newcomers were to become the ancestors of the berries that we enjoy today.

Jacques Cartier found abundant wild strawberries growing along the banks of the St. Lawrence River in 1534, and white strawberries were reported growing in the colonies of New York and Massachusetts two years later. The First Nations called the berry *wuttahimneash,* and "heart berry," believing that it strengthened the heart. They held feasts at the time of the harvest, and used it in every form of cooking and baking, including making bread. The newcomers used the terms "Virginia

strawberry," "meadow strawberry," and "scarlet strawberry" for it.

In 1607, Captain John Smith reported from Virginia:

Captain Newport and my selfe with divers other,
set forward to discover the [James] River, some fiftie
or sixtie miles, finding it in some places broader, and
in some narrower ... the people in all places kind-
ly treating us daunsing and feasting us with strawberries, Mulberies, Bread, Fish and other their
Countrie provisions ...

Roger Williams of Rhode Island marvelled at the great
size of the strawberries in his area — "four times bigger than
ours in England," was his description.

Meanwhile, Spanish explorers found natives in
Central and South America cultivating a very large berry
called *frutilla,* but paid scant attention to it until a French
naval engineer, Amede Frezier, rediscovered it in 1712
when he was exploring Ecuador and took some plants
home to France with him for the Royal Gardens in Paris
and Brittany. This berry was abundant on the Pacific coast
as far north as Alaska and on the Hawaiian Islands, and it
was eventually given the English name of "beach berry"
or "Chilean strawberry." Unfortunately, Frezier only took
female plants back to France and therefore they never
bore fruit. However, a few years later his plants were accidentally crossed with the earlier arrival, the Virginia strawberry, resulting in a large, fruited hybrid, one of which was

the celebrated Ananassa strawberry, and eventually the "Pineapple strawberry" or "pine strawberry."

Settlers arriving in Canada in the late eighteenth and early nineteenth centuries found an abundance of wild strawberries, and so did not consider cultivating them in the early years. In fact, President Martin Van Buren of the United States, who held office from 1837 to 1841 and who cultivated strawberries for his own enjoyment in his garden at the White House, was strongly criticized by his countrymen for his extravagance.

It was really in the middle of the nineteenth century, when Albany, New York horticulturist James Wilson developed a hardy "Wilson" variety, that cultivation could be considered seriously. When refrigerated rail cars were developed in the last quarter of the 1800s, the problem of transporting the perishable harvest across this vast continent quickly and safely was solved, and cultivation flourished. Communities large and small sponsored Strawberry Socials and Festivals annually, and housewives began experimenting with various methods of canning or preserving this fragile treat.

In 1904 the first strawberry sundae was created, and, of course, it took North America by storm as every local ice cream parlour on the continent developed its own version of this new sensation.

The twentieth century, with its improvements in home freezers, solved the dilemma of preservation for all types of fruit, including the strawberry. Despite these advances, and the development of bigger and better hybrids, many Canadians still prefer the wild strawberries found in the woods and along the roadsides and fencerows. They agree wholeheartedly with William Butler, who wrote in the 1600s in reference to the wild (not the hybrid) strawberry, "Doubtless God could have made a better berry, but doubtless God never did."

The best way to eat wild strawberries is in a deep dish, maybe with a little sifted sugar, and lots of champagne, claret, or white wine poured over them to bring out the flavour and act as an antiseptic. A favourite way to eat the cultivated fresh berry is to gently mash it with a fork, dust with sifted sugar, and pour on the cream.

Next in popularity to eating the berries in a bowl is the enduring and very Canadian dessert, strawberry shortcake. It was first recorded in the middle of the nineteenth century, and still continues in popularity today. The English term "shortcake" is usually synonymous with "shortbread" and was first mentioned by William Shakespeare in the *Merry Wives of Windsor* in 1598. In Canada, "shortcake" suitable for strawberries applies to a "short" dough, made with lard, butter, or other fat, that can be made into individual shortcakes or one large round, as it would have been in the nineteenth century. Early versions used pouring cream, rather than the whipping cream that we prefer nowadays.

Strawberry Shortcake
2 cups sifted flour
1/4 cup sugar
4 teaspoons baking powder
1/2 teaspoon salt

Stir well, and then add:
6 tablespoons butter

Mix well again until it is coarse and crumbly.
Then add, one at a time:
1 well beaten egg
1/3 cup milk

Mix well, and roll or pat into individual shortcakes,
or one large round. Place on a buttered cookie sheet
or other flat pan. Bake at 400°F for 10 minutes if
individual, or 15 to 20 minutes if a round. About an
hour before serving, wash, dry, and cut up one quart
of fresh strawberries, reserving several whole ones
for decoration. Add approximately 1/2 cup sugar
(either brown or white) to the cut-up berries and let
stand at room temperature. Split the shortcakes (butter them if desired), spoon on the berries and juice,
put on shortcake tops, and finish with whipped
cream and whole berries. Serve immediately.

If you only have a few berries and want to stretch
them to serve several people, you can do it by making this
delicious treat:

Strawberry Fool
Lightly crush your raw strawberries and sweeten
with a little brown sugar. Whip an equal amount of
whipping cream and gently fold the two together.

Do not be too thorough, so that there is a marbleized effect. Spoon gently into individual glass serving dishes and garnish each one with a slice of berry, a whole berry, or a sprig of mint. Keep refrigerated until ready to serve.

Another elegant dessert can be stretched to serve six:

Strawberries Romanoff
1 quart strawberries
1/2 cup brown sugar
1 cup sour cream

Wash, hull, and dry the berries. Slice into glass serving dishes. Combine sour cream and brown sugar and spoon gently over the sliced berries. Garnish with a sprig of mint or with berry slices and keep refrigerated. Serve within the hour, or the berries may begin to soften.

This, by the way, is a wonderful way to serve green grapes as well. Be sure to remove seeds.

Strawberries herald that short but wonderful period every summer when we can make Summer Pudding, and if you have never made it, this is your year! It is still a great favourite in Britain, but often the forgotten dessert in Canada:

Summer Pudding
1 loaf white bread (unsliced with the crust removed)
approximately 2 cups each of the following: strawberries, red currants, black currants, raspberries (other soft fruits can be substituted if you cannot find one of these four)
1 cup sugar
1/2 pint whipping cream

Cut the white bread into 1/4-inch slices and carefully line the bottom and sides of a bowl that will hold about a quart. Keep some of the bread to make a lid. Place the fruits and sugar in a saucepan and heat slowly until the sugar is just dissolved and the juice is beginning to ooze out of the fruit. Spoon the fruit and juice into the bowl, reserving a few spoons of juice in the refrigerator. Cover the top of the bowl with the remaining bread so that it forms a lid. Lay a saucer or plate and a weight of some kind over it to hold it in place. Refrigerate overnight. When ready to serve, remove the saucer and weight and turn out on a serving plate. Use the reserved juice to cover any spots of bread that are still white. Whip the cream and serve with the pudding, and be prepared to serve seconds.

As well as being good to eat, strawberries are good for us, as they are rich in both vitamins A and C. A handful of strawberries will provide an adult's daily requirement of vitamin C, and more vitamin A than the same weight of raisins. Their name comes from the Old English *streawberige,* perhaps because their runners resemble straw, but as far as taste is concerned they are closer to ambrosia.

Berry Delicious!

Hither soon as spring is fled, You and Charles and I will walk;
Lurking berries, ripe and red, Then will hang on every stalk
　　William Wordsworth, "Foresight"

Berries. The very word encourages visions of luscious fruit ripe for the picking, of juicy tarts and pies and jars of preserves. The ripe, plump fruits of the strawberry, raspberry, blackberry, mulberry, Saskatoon, elderberry, partridgeberry, foxberry, and gooseberry grace Canadian tables from June to September in every conceivable form — raw, stewed, baked into tarts, pies, and puddings, preserved in jams and jellies, and combined in ice cream, sorbet, and soup. In the late fall we even search for branches of berries that can be cut and added to decorative arrangements to brighten our homes over the winter.

Where did this love of berries begin? Historians tell us that it was probably 5000 B.C. when the Mesolithic peoples living in what is now Europe added wild berries they found in the forests to their regular diet of meat and fish. From then to the present we have continued to harvest and use berries to serve our needs, first from the wilds, and eventually from cultivated trees, shrubs, and plants.

118

It appears to be the Romans who left us the most complete records of how they were using berries in beverages, dyes, and medicines. During the Elizabethan period, popular walled gardens were the perfect place to cultivate and nurture many of the berries we know today — strawberries, hindberries (raspberries), gooseberries, and mulberries.

By the time the explorers, fur traders, and settlers arrived in Canada, both wild and cultivated berries of many kinds were an important part of their diet. To ensure they would have them available, they often brought plants and cuttings to transplant in what they called the New World. Here the newcomers met the First Nations, who also had been using berries for beverages, dyes, medicines, and food for centuries. What a sharing and exchange of information, advice, and caution there must have been between the two cultures! The newcomers found new and different varieties of berries, such as blueberries and cranberries, and learned from the First Nations those that were edible and those that were not. They learned new recipes for medicines and for cooling and soothing drinks to lessen fevers, ways to incorporate berries in food recipes, and methods to dry them so they would be preserved over the winter.

The newcomers brought with them their love of fruit tarts (pies) and puddings. They experimented with all the varieties that grew so abundantly in the wilds and integrated them into their traditional Old World recipes.

Berries enhance any recipe, but Canadians have traditionally shown a preference for fruit baked in pies. In the eighteenth and early nineteenth centuries the words "pie" and "tart" appear to have been interchangeable, so if you are researching early recipes do not be surprised to find that an Apple Tart is really an Apple Pie! For example, in *Ancient Cookery*, published in 1381, we find this recipe:

For to make Tartys in Apples:
Take good apples and good spices & Figs and raisins and pears and when they are well braid colour with safron well and do it in a coffin and do it forth to bake well.

Canadians have developed many regional favourites, depending on our location and the availability of berries. The partridgeberry is a favourite in Newfoundland:

Old-fashioned Partridgeberry Tart
2 cups fresh or frozen partridgeberries
1 cup sugar
2 tablespoons cornstarch
1/8 teaspoon salt

Combine these ingredients and bring slowly to a boil, stirring constantly. Cook until thickened. Add:

1 tablespoon butter
1/2 teaspoon vanilla

Cool and place in an 8-inch pastry shell. Decorate with a lattice of pastry and bake in a moderate oven

of 350°F for about 25 minutes. Cool and serve
with cream.

A modern version can be made by omitting the
lattice of pastry on top and, when it is baked, making
a meringue by beating 2 egg whites and 4 tablespoons
of sugar until stiff. Spread meringue over the cool filling in the pie shell. Bake in a moderate 325°F oven
for about 20 minutes or until golden brown.

Saskatoon berries (after which the city of Saskatoon was
named) grow in the region stretching from the western
provinces to Manitoulin Island in Ontario. These succulent
berries can be used in many recipes as well as in pies.

Saskatoon Berry Pie
4 cups fresh or frozen Saskatoon berries
1/2 cup sugar
4 tablespoons flour
1/4 teaspoon salt
1/4 cup cooking sherry or wine

Combine sugar, flour, and salt. Place half the berries
on a pastry-lined pie plate and sprinkle with half
the mixture. Add remaining berries and cover with
remaining mixture. Pour on sherry or wine. Cover
with pastry top and seal. Make large open designs in
pastry for steam to emerge. Bake at 425°F for 20
minutes, then reduce to 375°F for 40 minutes.

For centuries before European contact, the First Nations made pemmican by mixing dried, crushed berries — Saskatoons, cranberries, and blueberries — with fat and dried elk, deer, or buffalo meat. This mixture was stored in leather bags and provided nourishment for the First Nations; with the arrival of explorers and fur traders it became an item of barter. It was a light, easily portable, and highly nutritious food — the perfect solution to sustain men engaged in long journeys by land and water in search of the elusive furs in the Canadian interior. Pemmican could be eaten cold, or boiling water could be poured over it to make a soup called "rubbaboo."

During the lean years of settlement in the prairies, cranberries were called the prairie cherry and were frequently baked in mock cherry pies.

Despite our changing Canadian landscape, clumps of elder shrubs still survive in many areas. Their masses of creamy white flowers in late May and early June can be used in teas, wine, muffins, and many other recipes. The heavy clusters of purple–black berries are ready to be harvested in late summer, and there are few fruits that can generate such nostalgia as this.

Elderberry Pie
Pastry for 2-crust pie
3 1/2 cups washed, stemmed elderberries
1 tablespoon lemon juice
1 cup sugar
1/4 teaspoon salt

1/2 cup flour
1 tablespoon butter

Spread elderberries in pastry-lined 9-inch pie pan.
Sprinkle with lemon juice. Combine sugar, salt, and
flour; sprinkle over berries. Dot with butter. Cover
top with pastry and seal. Cut vents in top crust.
Bake at 400°F, 35–45 minutes or until juices show
in vents and crust is golden brown.

Finally, if you want to enjoy summer fruits and haven't
time to make a pie, make a Fool instead! Take two cups of the
fruit of your choice and simmer gently, adding sugar to taste.
Cool. Take equal amounts of stewed fruit and whipped cream
and mix gently. Spoon into individual glass serving dishes.
Garnish with a walnut, cherry, mint leaf, or whatever. Store in
the refrigerator until ready to serve. Your guests will think that
you worked hard on that one, so bask in their compliments.

Bountiful Blueberries

*Berry Pickin' time — when hearts were light and baskets were heavy —
with Blueberries. What joy!*
Beatrice Ross Ruszek, *The Blueberry Connection*

Blueberries have been an important addition to North American diets for centuries. Native North Americans were eating wild blueberries long before the first arrivals from the Old World.

Early travellers to British North America noted in their diaries the diverse ways that blueberries were used. In 1618, when Samuel de Champlain travelled among the Huron Nation, he described them gathering blueberries for winter use:

> After drying berries in the sun, the Indians beat them into powder and added this powder to parched meal to make a dish called Sautauthig. We found it to be delicious.

Blueberries grew profusely in the eastern regions of the continent, and Natives added them to their breads, soups, stews, puddings, fish, and meat. As well as eating them raw and in cooked dishes, the First Nations often created pigments from berries, and they knew that a rich brown dye resulted from mixing blueberries with nuts.

As the fur trade developed in North America, the First Nations bartered pemmican for the trade goods offered by both the individual traders and the giant fur trade companies.

The popular succulent wild blueberries grew in a low, dense carpet called a barrens; they thrived in sandy or rocky acidic soil and produced small, tart fruit. For the new arrivals on Canadian shores the blueberry was not a stranger, for they knew similar berries in England and Europe called bilberries, whortleberries, or huckleberries, and of course the Scots knew the blaeberry of their homeland. There are many recipes in which these berries can be used interchangeably.

The First Nations taught the newcomers how to dry blueberries for winter and also how to make strengthening medicines and tonics from the juice, so they were not only a seasonal food and flavouring but a year-round medicine and restorative. Modern research has proven how true these beliefs in their medicinal properties were. In many parts of Canada where blueberries were abundant, annual traditions developed around the harvest. Favourite pails, dippers, and baskets went year after year to the blueberry barrens with the pickers (often the whole family was involved), and once there each person staked out an area as his or her own. The day was then spent in picking and also exchanging the news of the neighbourhood. Social events were organized around the days of picking so that it became a season of festivity and fellowship.

As well as the recipes and medicines that they learned from the First Nations, the colonists developed a host of simple, straightforward, and practically foolproof recipes for using this abundant fruit. Having stood the test of time, these recipes are mute witnesses to the magic quality of blueberries.

Today Canadians can choose between the two native blueberries: the lowbush, which thrives in the wild and has been a part of our diet for so long, or the relative newcomer the highbush, which was cultivated in the twentieth century with a characteristic large, sweet berry. The fruit can be interchanged in recipes, although many Canadian cooks are staunchly loyal to only one or the other. The more we learn about blueberries the more we realize that there are few foods in the Canadian kitchen that evoke so many memories and nostalgic remembrances and such devotion as this modest little blue fruit.

Doughboys with Blueberry Sauce
1 cup granulated sugar
1/2 cup water
1 quart blueberries

Make a syrup of the sugar and water by boiling for 5 minutes. Add blueberries and boil until tender, but do not overcook.

To make Doughboys:
2 cups flour sifted with 3 teaspoons baking powder
1/4 teaspoon salt
1 tablespoon butter
1 tablespoon sugar

Mix all the ingredients and cut in butter. Add 2/3 cup milk or water, sufficient to make dough. Drop from a tablespoon into the blueberry mixture. Cover and cook rapidly for 15 minutes with the cover on. Serve hot with whipped cream.

A basic cake recipe that can be served plain, iced, or with whipped cream comes from *St. Luke's Cook Book*, published in Winnipeg, Manitoba in 1910 to support their fundraising drive for a new church organ:

Blueberry Cake
One pint flour, one cup milk, one-fourth cup butter, one cup sugar, one cup berries, two teaspoons baking powder: cream sugar, butter and flour; add fourth of cup of melted butter, fold through and put in white of one egg; last flour, berries, milk.

Although the recipe gives us no hint about how to bake, I recommend that you mix all ingredients well, grease an 8-inch square pan, pour in batter, and bake at 375°F for about 35 minutes or until, when tested with toothpick, it comes out clean and dry.

Blueberry Grunt
4 cups blueberries
1/2 cup water
1/2 cup sugar

2 cups flour
1 teaspoon sugar
1/2 teaspoon salt
2 teaspoons baking powder
1 tablespoon butter
milk

Boil berries, water, and 1/2 cup sugar until juice comes out of the fruit. Pour into a greased baking dish. Sift dry ingredients together, then cut in 1 tablespoon butter and enough milk to dampen the dough. Roll out gently into a crust to fit the baking dish, secure well around the edge, and bake for about 15 minutes at 350°F.

A French Canadian Cookbook by Donald Asselin, published in 1968, shares with us this tip about blueberry pies:

They are especially delicious if brushed with butter and sprinkled with a mixture of 2 tablespoons sugar, 1/4 teaspoon nutmeg, and 1/2 teaspoon grated lemon rind. My grandfather had a slab of one of these berry pies every morning for breakfast with a cup of scalding hot tea and a cucumber when in season.

Readers may want to try this refinement on the following basic recipe:

Blueberry Pie

Make your favourite pie crust for a two-crust pie or use the following recipe:

Pastry
2 generous cups flour
pinch of salt
1/2 cup shortening
ice cold water

Cut the shortening into the flour and mix well. Mix with a fork or your hands until crumbly. Add a pinch of salt and then the ice water slowly until pastry clings together and is ready to roll. Reserve a third of the pastry for the top. Spread 1 tablespoon of flour on the bottom crust to avoid soaking.

Filling
4 cups blueberries
3/4 cup sugar
2 tablespoons flour mixed with the sugar

Fill pastry-lined pie plate with the fruit and the sugar and flour mixture. Be sure the pie crust rim is higher than the fruit to avoid boiling over. Roll out the remaining dough into a large circle to lay on the fruit. Pierce in several places or cut a design in the pastry to allow the steam to rise. Bake at 400°F for

10 minutes and then reduce to 350°F for approximately 30 minutes. Serve cold, either plain or garnished with ice cream or whipped cream.

Puddings of all kinds, both savoury and sweet, have been great favourites with Canadians for centuries, and from *Tried and True Recipes*, published by St. Andrew's United Church in Kingston circa 1900, comes an easy recipe and a suggested variation:

Blueberry Pudding
3/4 cup sugar
1/4 cup butter
2 cups flour
3 teaspoons baking powder
1/2 teaspoon salt
3/4 cup milk
1 egg
2 cups blueberries (lightly dusted with flour)

Mix all the ingredients in a bowl, adding floured blueberries last. Bake at 350°F or steam in a chimney mould. Serve with sauce or whipped cream.

Another way would be, one cup of milk, half teaspoon of soda dissolved in it, one cup molasses, one pint of blueberries, flour enough to make a pretty thick batter. Steam two hours.

A Bowl of Cherries

So we grew together, Like to a double cherry, seeming parted,
But yet an union in partition — Two lovely berries moulded on one stem.
William Shakespeare, *A Midsummer-Night's Dream*

Cherry trees were probably native to the Mediterranean area. The word "cherry" comes from the Greek *kerasos,* which became *chery* in Middle English. In Roman times, cherries were preserved whole by immersing them, stems and all, in honey, to be served as a dessert or sweetmeat. The Romans are credited with taking cherries to Britain, and from there they quickly spread to the four corners of the earth.

When newcomers from Great Britain and Europe arrived in North America, they found the First Nations already using wild black cherries for food and medicine. The cherries were eaten raw or dried for winter use. Sometimes they were cooked, formed into small cakes, dried, and stored in birch bark containers. When medicines were needed, cherries were an important ingredient. The root of the cherry was boiled and a decoction taken internally for worms, ulcers, and cholera or used externally as a disinfectant wash for cuts and wounds.

Many First Nations would not drink water that they encountered in their travels unadulterated, always boiling it

131

first and often adding leaves or bark to the liquid. A favourite combination involved the bark of black cherry and chokecherry. The twigs and bark were tied in little bundles and dropped into boiling water; the mixture would be sweetened with maple sugar and drunk while hot.

The cherries that early settlers used were probably a variation of the wild red cherry tree, a small species with lance-shaped leaves and clusters of white flowers, found growing in sunny locations from Newfoundland to British Columbia. In temperate climes it would begin flowering in April, with the promise of fruit in July or August, depending on the area. The newcomers began cultivating the wild cherries and crossbreeding them with European varieties. The fruit was popular for pies, puddings, and preserved with maple sugar or raw or refined sugar as a dessert fruit. Cherry pie was, and is, an all-time favourite. It was so popular in the late nineteenth and early twentieth centuries, in fact, that many cookbooks contained recipes for mock cherry pie, made from raisins and cranberries in regions where cherries were not readily available.

Today, there are two types of cherry — sweet and sour (also referred to as tart). Both can be used as a cooking fruit, but only sweet cherries, of which there are about six hundred known varieties, are eaten as is. There are around three hundred varieties of sour cherry, of which the Bing, developed in 1875 by a farmer in Milwaukee, Oregon, is perhaps the best known.

In Canada, cherries are in season for only a short period during the summer, but that doesn't mean doing without them for the rest of the year. Frozen and canned cherries are always readily available and can be successfully incorporated into almost every course, from soups to liqueurs and everything in between. Here are two historic recipes and several modern ones for you to try:

Canned Cherries
Ingredients: to every 1 pound of fruit, 1/2 pound of sugar, 3 gills [1/2 pint] of water.

Put the sugar and water on the fire to heat, and as soon as it comes to a boil put in the cherries and only allow them to scald for a quarter of an hour; put into bottles boiling hot and seal. A few of the kernels [cherry pits] put in to scald with the fruit imparts a fine flavour. Note: Be sure to skim well.
The Dominion Cook Book, Anne Clarke, 1899.

Cherry Pie
Line your pie plate with good crust, fill half full with ripe cherries; sprinkle over them about a cupful of sugar, a teaspoon of sifted flour, dot a few bits of butter over that. Now fill the crust full to the top. Cover with the upper crust and bake. For every cherry pie the under crust should be well coated with the white of an egg; when the under crust is prepared and baked in this way it is crispy, brown and tender, instead of sodden, as the under crusts of such pies too often are, and the pie, when done, readily slips

off the plate. The best way to egg pastry is to turn
the whole white of an egg over it, allowing it to pass
over every portion; then turning it off. When the
white of an egg is used in this way one white will
be sufficient to egg three or four pies.

Mrs. Flynn's Cookbook by Katherine Lewis Flynn,
first published as a fundraiser for the St. Elizabeth's
Aid Society of St. Vincent's Orphanage in Prince
Edward Island in 1930

Cherry Soup
1 pound sweet cherries (canned or frozen black
cherries may be substituted)
2 1/2 cups water
1/2 cup white sugar
1 cinnamon stick
1/4 cup water
2 tablespoons corn starch
1 cup red wine
1 cup rich cream
1/4 teaspoon almond extract

Pit the cherries and combine with sugar, cinnamon
stick, and 2 1/2 cups water in a saucepan. Cover and
simmer for about 5 minutes. Remove the cherries
and the cinnamon stick. Combine 1/4 cup of water
and 2 tablespoons corn starch. Add to the cherry
liquid and simmer for an additional 3 or 4 minutes.
Let cool completely and then stir in as gently as

possible the wine, cream, and almond extract. Chill for several hours. When ready to serve, this soup can be garnished with a dollop of whipped cream and a sprinkle of cinnamon.

Cherry Pancakes
4 crusty white rolls
4 tablespoons all-purpose flour
2 eggs
1 cup milk
4 tablespoons white sugar
1 pound fresh pitted cherries
butter
cinnamon sugar

Place the rolls in a bowl, cover with cold water, and let stand until thoroughly soaked. Squeeze rolls dry and break up. Add flour, eggs, milk, sugar, and pitted cherries. Mix well. These may be deep fried in shortening or salad oil, or fried in butter in the traditional way. Make them small to ensure they cook well, sprinkle with cinnamon sugar and serve.

Cherry Sauce
1/4 cup fresh lemon juice
6 strips lemon rind (about 2 inches long)
6 strips orange rind (about 2 inches long)
1 cinnamon stick
2 1/2 cups red wine (preferably dry)

1 1/4 cup sugar
1 pound sweet cherries (stems and pits removed)

Combine lemon juice, lemon and orange rind, cinnamon stick, wine, and sugar in a heavy saucepan.
Bring to a boil, stirring, and simmer for 5 or 6 minutes. Add the cherries and simmer again for about
15 minutes. Lift the cherries out and save in a bowl.
Discard the lemon and orange rind and cinnamon
stick. Heat the liquid over high heat and reduce the
liquid to about 1 1/4 cups. Pour over the cherries
and let it cool before serving.

Cherries Jubilee
1 1/2 pints vanilla ice cream
1 can Bing cherries, pitted
1/3 cup black currant jelly
1/4 cup brandy

Scoop the ice cream out of the container, wrap
each scoop in foil, and put in freezer. Place the
black currant jelly and cherries in a chafing dish or
an electric frying pan, stirring constantly until the
jelly melts and the mixture simmers. Pour the
brandy in the middle of the fruit, but do not stir!
Heat for a few seconds and then carefully hold a
lighted match over the spot where you poured the
brandy. While the cherries flame, pour over the ice
cream and serve.

A Bowl of Cherries

Cherry Charlotte

3 tablespoons butter
8 slices dry bread (French bread if possible)
1/4 cup white sugar
1 pound Bing cherries
1/2 cup water
1/2 cup brown sugar
2 teaspoons lemon juice
1 cinnamon stick
4 tablespoons rum or rum extract

Butter the bread on both sides. Sprinkle with sugar on one side and brown on both sides in a frying pan over low heat. Place in a shallow dish. Wash, drain, pit, and remove stems from cherries. Boil the water, brown sugar, lemon juice, and cinnamon. Add cherries and simmer for about 4 minutes. Remove the cinnamon. Add the rum or extract and pour over bread in a shallow bowl. Serve warm with ice cream or whipped cream. This recipe can be varied by adding any fresh, uncooked fruit to the cherries when they are removed from the heat.

In Praise
of the Peach

An apple is an excellent thing — until you have tried a peach.
George du Maurier

Our love affair with the peach begins each spring when millions of Canadians are lured to the orchards, especially in the Niagara Peninsula or the Okanagan Valley, where the beautiful soft pink blossoms hold centre stage. From early summer to the first frost in the autumn our infatuation grows as baskets of peaches beckon to us from roadside stands, from our grocers' displays, and from billboard and magazine advertisements.

Originally a native of China, the peach spread along the caravan routes of Asia, then to the countries surrounding the Mediterranean Sea and thus to Europe. Chinese writings refer to *tao* — the peach — as early as the fifth century B.C. It is believed that the Greeks and the Romans were cultivating peach trees and that they eventually introduced them to the countries under their influence.

Spanish explorers brought the first peaches to North America as early as 1600 when they visited Florida and Mexico. The First Nations were so fond of peaches that they began cultivating them in their villages and carrying them north along the eastern seaboard as far as the climate allowed. When the early settlers arrived they were surprised to see the abundance of peach trees under cultivation, and William Penn commented on this in 1683 when he noted that although some of the fruit was of poor quality, it certainly was abundant. On July 2, 1793, while living at Navy Hall at Niagara, Elizabeth Graves Simcoe, wife of the first lieutenant-governor of Upper Canada, confirmed the natives' love of peaches:

> The Indians are particularly fond of fruit. We have thirty large May Duke cherry trees behind the house, and three standard peach trees, which supplied us last autumn for tarts and desserts during six weeks, beside the numbers the young men eat. My share was trifling compared with theirs, and I eat thirty in a day. They were very small and high flavoured. When tired of eating them raw, Mr. Talbot roasted them and they were very good.

Peach culture began to boom in North America in the nineteenth century when William Crawford of New Jersey developed two new varieties of peaches, one known as "Crawford's Late" and another as "Crawford's Early," a freestone peach with "melting yellow flesh and luscious flavour" that took the market by storm and became the leading seller commercially until the middle of the nineteenth century.

By 1917 there were over two thousand varieties of peaches in North America; however, it was eventually the

Elberta that became the all-time favourite because of its hardiness and productivity. Peach culture is attended by great risks, particularly on this continent with its wildly fluctuating climate, as the buds and blossoms are easily killed by late frosts and even the winter buds may be killed by severe weather.

Peaches grow best in sandy soil, and since the lake regions provide this, as well as moderating the climate and protecting against frosts, peaches were, and are, an ideal fruit to cultivate in areas such as the Niagara Peninsula (which accounts for some 90 percent of production) and the Okanagan Valley. As well as demanding certain soil and climatic conditions, the peach tree is very vulnerable to insects and a host of fungi and bacterial diseases. Before the advent of modern sprays, many methods of controlling the problems were popular:

Hanging Mothballs on Your Peach Tree
We carefully sprayed our peach against leaf curl, and still the leaves curled. "Pick off the affected leaves and hang a few moth balls on the tree" we were told. No more leaf curl that year, but to guard against a reputation for eccentricity, the reason for decorating a peach tree like a Christmas tree in the summer with white balls or pretty mauve Mothax rings should be explained to visitors!

The Source Book, published in Winnipeg and Toronto in 1924, confirmed to its readers that "the peach is too well known to need description" and that "peaches are placed upon the market fresh, canned or dried." Our Canadian ancestors used them in every possible way — eaten fresh (in season), preserved in a sugar syrup or in spirits as a dessert, distilled into brandy, made into pickles or puddings (sometimes called flummeries), or crystallized as a sweetmeat to eat at the end of a meal.

For those housewives attempting to preserve them in their own kitchens, stone crocks were used, often sealed shut with a bladder. In the nineteenth century the advent of preserving jars and the use of wax as a sealer was a great boon to the home canner. *Mrs. Clarke's Cookery Book* gives us a number of recipes for preserving peaches that can still be used today:

Canning Peaches

First prepare the syrup. For canned fruits, one quart of granulated sugar to two quarts of water is the proper proportion; to be increased or lessened according to the quantity of fruit to be canned, but always twice as much water as sugar. Use a porcelain kettle, and, if possible, take care that it is kept solely for canning and preserving — nothing else.

Pour hot water over the peaches and the skin will come off; drop into cold water to prevent them changing colour. As soon as the syrup has come to a boil, put in the peaches allow them to boil till tender. Try them with a broom straw and if tender, place in hot bottles, pour over the boiling syrup to nearly running over and seal immediately.

Peaches in Brandy
Ingredients: 1/4 pound of sugar to 1 pound of fruit, brandy.

Wipe, weigh, and pick the fruit, and have ready the fine sugar in fine powder. Put the fruit into an ice pot that shuts very close; throw the sugar over it, and then cover the fruit with brandy. Between the top and cover of the pot put a piece of double cap paper. Set the pot into a saucepan of water until the brandy be as hot as you can bear to put your finger in, but it must not boil. Put the fruit into a jar, and pour the brandy on it. When cold, put a bladder over, and tie it down tightly.

Sweet Peach Pickle
Ingredients: To 4 pounds of peaches allow 2 pounds of white sugar, 1/2 ounce of each of mace, cinnamon and cloves mixed, and 1 pint of the best white vinegar.

Pour scalding water over the peaches and remove the skins with a butter knife; drop into cold water; stick four cloves in each peach. Lay the peaches in preserving pan with the sugar sprinkled over them; bring gradually to the boil, add vinegar and spice, boil five or six minutes. Remove the peaches and place in bottles. Boil the syrup thick and pour over boiling hot.

In Praise of the Peach

The Great Nineteenth Century Household Guide by Grandma Nichols, 1894, like so many of its counterparts, gave the housewife not only recipes but also invaluable advice on how to look after her canning equipment, jars, and other matters of domestic importance:

Cleaning Fruit Jars
A handful of carpet tacks will clean fruit jars or bottles readily. Half fill the jars with hot soapsuds, put in the tacks, cover, give vigorous shaking, and rinse well.

Peach Jelly
Pare, stone, and slice the peaches, crack some of the stones and remove the kernels, put the peaches and kernels into a jar and stand the jar in a pot of boiling water, stir frequently pressing the fruit against the sides of the jar; when it is well broken strain, and allow the juice of a lemon to every pint of juice, mix and allow one pound of sugar to one pint of juice, put the juice on to simmer half an hour, then add the sugar hot; allow it just to come to a boil, and remove from the fire; allow to get cold; cover with paper soaked in brandy, then with paper brushed with the white of an egg.

Flummeries were eighteenth- and nineteenth-century dishes that we seldom hear about today. A flummery was usually a soft, jelly-like dessert, often combining a cereal (such as cooked oatmeal) with fruit and nuts. *The New Galt Cook Book* gives us a recipe for a good peach flummery:

Peach Flummery
Line the bottom of a glass or porcelain dish with stale cake, not more than an inch and a half thick. Make a boiled custard out of a pint of milk and the yolks of four eggs, and just before serving pour it over the cake. On this spread a thick layer of peeled, sliced and sugared peaches, and over that a meringue made of the whites of four eggs beaten stiff, with four tablespoons of sugar.

In Canada today, peaches are available to us all year round, and using modern convenience foods, savoury desserts can be prepared quickly and easily at any time of the year.

Fruit Flan
These flat cakes or pies (often called tarts in the past centuries) are of Germanic origin and are becoming increasingly popular in Canada. They can be easily made.

Make your favourite pastry or use ready-mixed pastry to line a large 9-inch pie plate, a flan ring, or a quiche pan, and bake.
Prepare a vanilla pudding mix according to instructions. Pour pudding into the cool pastry shell. Use canned peaches, pears, oranges, cherries,

or other fruit that has been well drained on a paper towel to create a pleasing spiral of fruits on the custard.

Make a glaze by combining 4 tablespoons of apple jelly or red currant jelly with 4 tablespoons of fruit flavoured liqueur. Heat in a saucepan and brush over the fruit. Refrigerate for 2 to 3 hours before serving. Serve plain or with whipped cream.

Bring Back the Beet!

The beet is the most intense of vegetables. The radish, admittedly, is more feverish, but the fire of the radish is a cold fire, the fire of discontent, not of passion.

Tom Robbins, author

A native of the Mediterranean area, the beet (or beet-root, as it is also known) was familiar to the ancients and was often mentioned in the writings of both Greeks and Romans. They appear to have eaten the leaves originally; the root didn't become part of their diet until sometime during the Christian era. The beet was one of the plants that Charlemagne wanted cultivated in his domains, but his wishes appear to have been ignored, for the vegetable had to be reintroduced to France during the Renaissance. The red beet that we know today was probably first culti-vated in Germany. With its high tolerance for salty soil, the beet later become ideal for planting on land reclaimed from the sea in both Italy and Holland. As it spread across Europe and Great Britain, it was incorporated into many other established recipes, such as this one from *The Experienced English House-Keeper*, Elizabeth Raffald, 1769, which has been modernized for your convenience:

Beetroot Pancakes
"A pretty corner dish for dinner or supper"
6 ounces peeled, cooked beets (fresh or canned)
2 tablespoons brandy
3 tablespoons whipping cream
4 egg yolks
3 tablespoons flour
2 teaspoons fine white sugar
1 teaspoon grated nutmeg
butter

Mash cooked beets as finely as possible and mix with the other ingredients (or put in your blender). Heat butter in a frying pan and drop the beet mixture into it. Shake the pan gently if the mixture needs to be flattened. Keep heat low as these will burn easily, and turn over as they cook quickly. You may want to wipe your pan with a paper towel between batches. These are good hot or cold, garnished with whipped cream, maple syrup, or preserves.

In the mid-eighteenth century, a German chemist, Andreas Sigismund Marggraf, discovered sugar in beetroot. Some fifty years later, Napoleon brought the sugar beet to prominence when the English blockaded France, cutting it off from its sources of cane sugar. Napoleon ordered that seventy thousand acres be planted with sugar beets, and in 1812 a French financier, Benjamin Delessert, opened a refinery in Paris to process the beets. Sugar beets subsequently became the second major source of the world's sugar supply because, unlike sugarcane, they could be grown in temperate or cool climates.

New arrivals in Canada soon discovered that beets were ideal for our climate as well, and they added colour and flavour to a diet that was too often bland and predictable. The fresh, young leaves could be used in salads, while older leaves were steamed or boiled, either on their own or with other vegetables. The roots could be boiled or baked and eaten hot or cold, often chopped in salads. Pickled beets were a staple on Canadian tables, and the basic recipes for preparing them appear in almost every cookbook from the nineteenth century to the present:

Pickled Beets
Choose a quantity of small beets (not larger than a golf ball). Wash carefully without piercing the skin as they will bleed. Cut off the tops, leaving about 1 inch of stem. Leave the roots on. Boil until tender and carefully slip off the skin with your fingers. While still warm, place in sterilized jars. (You may prefer to slice or cube the beets rather than leaving them whole.) Meanwhile, prepare enough liquid to cover in the following quantities:

3 cups water
8 cups vinegar
6 cups brown sugar
2 tablespoons salt

Bring Back the Beet!

Bring just to the boiling point but do not boil. Pour over the cooked and peeled beets in the sterilized jars. Seal.

Many cultural groups brought their own favourite recipes. For example, over 170,000 new arrivals from the Ukraine, Poland, and Germany settled in Canada in the late nineteenth century, many of them in our western provinces. This one comes to us from the Manitoba Historical Society, publishers of *Manitoba's Heritage Cookery*, 1992:

Borscht
8 cups water
2 to 3 cups grated potatoes
3 cups shredded cabbage
1 medium onion, chopped fine
4 1/2 cups almost cooked beets (slip skin off), shredded or grated
1 1/2 cups canned or fresh tomatoes
1 14-ounce can pork and beans
1/2 cup sugar (add more, if you would like it sweeter)
1/2 cup vinegar
1/2 cup chicken soup base
2 tablespoons fresh dill (finely cut up)
2 tablespoons salt

Bring water, potatoes, cabbage, and onion to a full boil; reduce heat and simmer until vegetables are cooked and tender. Add remaining ingredients. Simmer for about 20 to 30 minutes, just to blend the flavours.

Through the centuries, the beet has been prized not only for its sugar content and as a food for humans and animals, but also as an important medicinal plant. Beet juice has been used as a shampoo to cure dandruff, while poultices of mashed beets were used as a remedy for inflamed eyes. Cooked beets were even used as an antidote for jaundice. People have long believed that beets are healthful because they "strengthen the blood," and modern science has found some truth in the claim: both roots and leaves contain vitamin C, potassium, and iron, while the greens also contain calcium and fibre.

Here are a few suggestions, if you are preparing beets for the first time:

- When choosing beets at the grocery store or market, the smaller the better. Look for firm, light-skinned beets with crisp, fresh leaves. If you are growing them, harvest them while they are small (golf ball sized or slightly larger).
- To store beets, cut off the tops about 1 inch from the beet. Do not cut off the roots. Beets should keep in a cool, dry place or refrigerator for 2 to 3 weeks.
- Store beets and beet leaves separately and use the leaves as soon as possible as they will wilt and become soggy within 2 to 3 days.

Bring Back the Beet!

- Unless the recipe calls for it, do not cut, peel, or pierce beets before using them in recipes, as they will bleed; a gentle wash to get rid of dirt is sufficient.
- Use beets of the same size in your recipes so they will cook evenly.
- Test cooked beets by trying to remove skin with your fingers. If it does not slip off easily, return to heat.

Beets can be prepared in many ways, by boiling, baking, steaming, roasting, and even grilling. They can be served hot or cold, with or without garnishes. They are fairly easy to grow and can also be purchased canned at the grocery store, either whole or sliced. Best of all, beet recipes are generally simple and forgiving. Why not bring back the beet and redis-cover the many ways you can enjoy this traditional vegetable?

Beet Salad
3 large cooked, fresh beets (or 1 can diced beets)
2 large stalks celery, diced
1 Spanish onion or 1 red onion, diced
mayonnaise or salad dressing of your choice

Put beets, celery, and onion in a salad bowl and add enough dressing to coat lightly. Marinate in refrig-erator for at least 1 hour before serving.

Sweet Beets
12 small new beets, boiled with skins off
3 tablespoons butter

2 tablespoons lemon juice
1 tablespoons honey
1/4 cup sour cream
salt and pepper to taste

Grate the cooked and peeled beets into a saucepan or casserole. Add the other ingredients and stir well. Place in a low oven at 300°F or stir over low heat until well blended and hot. Serves 5 or 6.

Spring Salad
12 small new beets, boiled with skins off
12 tiny new potatoes, boiled separately with skins on
2 stalks celery, washed
selection of washed greens — fresh, young dandelion leaves, beet leaves, parsley, mint, etc.
1 clove garlic, peeled and chopped finely
salt to taste
dressing of extra virgin olive oil and red wine vinegar

Slice beets and potatoes as thin as possible and celery into thin strips. Combine all ingredients and herbs in a bowl, dress with oil and vinegar. Add garlic. Add salt to taste.

Dorothy's Beet Chutney
6 medium-sized beets, boiled and peeled
1 apple, peeled and chopped
1 large cooking onion, peeled and chopped

Bring Back the Beet!

1 cup brown sugar
1 cup cider vinegar
1 cup seedless raisins
1/4 cup candied ginger, diced
1/2 cup apricots
salt and pepper to taste

Dice the cooked, peeled beets into a slow cooker or large saucepan (not aluminum). Add chopped apples, onions, and all other ingredients. Bring to a boil if in a saucepan and then lower heat. Simmer for about an hour, or until thickened. Ladle into sterilized jars, seal, and store in the refrigerator if you plan to use the chutney within the next month. If you plan to keep it longer, process jars in a boiling water bath for about 30 minutes to preserve. This can easily be made in a slow cooker and will take from 3 to 4 hours to finish. Makes about four 8-ounce jars.

Know Your Onions

Happy is said to be the family which can eat onions together. They are, for the time being, separate from the world, and have a harmony of aspiration.
Charles Dudley Warner, "My Summer in a Garden"

The onion is such a common vegetable today that we often overlook it for more exotic or cosmopolitan offerings in our markets and local stores. We should remember, however, that the onion, along with its mild and sweet cousin the leek, has a long and proud history, for it has been cultivated since at least 3000 B.C. A native of Asia and Africa, it was worshipped by the ancient Egyptians — they, along with the Babylonians, believed that the onion was a symbol of perfection because it has a circular shape and one can travel the line around a circle to eternity. For this reason a bouquet of onions was placed in the mummies' hands to assist them through the afterlife.

The children of Israel mourned the loss of the onion and its flavourful relatives after they left Egypt, for we read in the Holy Bible, Numbers 11: "We remember the fish, which we did eat in Egypt freely; the cucumbers, and the melons, and the leeks, and the onions, and the garlic." To show how highly these herbs were esteemed, it is recorded that in 484 B.C. there was an inscription on the Great Pyramid stating that a sum of sixteen hundred talents had been paid for supplying the workmen with onions. By the beginning of the Christian era the onion was so sacred in Egypt that the priests forbade it being eaten, and scholars such as Horace, Pliny, and Xenophon were among those who paid tribute to it in writing. It was probably the Romans who introduced onions and leeks to the British Isles, where for over a thousand years the leek has been the popular national plant of Wales. Legends tell us that during a victory by the last Briton King, Cadwallader, over the Saxons in 640, the Welsh wore leeks in their hats to distinguish themselves from the enemy and to bring them good luck.

Through the centuries, many types of onions have emerged. Generally, the warmer the climate, the larger the onion and the milder its taste. In colder regions, onions are harder and more strongly flavoured and they keep longer. Among the better known are: the mild Bermuda and Spanish; the early Potato or Underground that can be harvested as early as July; the Egyptian, which produces small bulbs instead of flowers and larger bulbs at the roots; and the perennial Welsh, which is really of Siberian origin and produces small leeks with chive-like leaves. There are hard but good onions known as Polish, and a flat, difficult-to-peel one called the Canary.

Over time, onions have become the most indispensable flavouring for cooks around the world. They may be eaten raw, pickled, boiled, stuffed, fried, mashed, baked, roasted, braised, or glazed. They have appeared in salads, stews, soups, sauces, gravies, omelettes, as a vegetable in their own right

— and even in porridge, as in this recipe from *The Cook's Guide*, published in 1884:

Onion Porridge
Take a Spanish onion as big as you can procure, peel and split into quarters, and put these into a small stewpan with a pint of water, a pat of butter, and a little salt; boil gently for half an hour; add a pinch of pepper, and eat the porridge just before retiring to bed. This is also an excellent remedy for colds, and was imparted to me by a jolly, warm hearted Yorkshire farmer.

As this recipe illustrates, the onion and its relatives were not only important foods and flavourings, but they were also attributed with medicinal properties. *The Household Guide or Domestic Cyclopedia*, published in 1894, leaves us with no doubt about the advantages of this vegetable:

The Useful Onion
The medicinal qualities of the onion are not to be despised. An onion will cure the earache quicker than any other remedy. Take two or three good sized onions. Peel them and cut in thin slices. Lay the slices on a cloth and heat until hot. Bind this to the head, letting it expand beyond the ear at least one inch all the way around. An Onion poultice is most useful in cases of internal inflammation, and onions are an excellent remedy for diphtheria and pneumonia.

When the digestive system is apt to become overloaded with rich, greasy or sweet foods, plenty of onions should be eaten as a counter balance. They are good for the stomach, the complexion, and the nerves when eaten either boiled or raw, but of course the unpleasant odour left on the breath after indulgence in them is a barrier to their use to many people who would otherwise be able to take advantage of the good there is in them. To overcome all this and give every one a chance, an old remedy is suggested — parsley. To entirely destroy the bad odour of onions eat a small sprig of this pretty green herb either with your meals or immediately after them. There will be nothing in the breath or about the person at all suggestive of the odoriferous bulb five minutes after the parsley is eaten.

This last tip would be of particular interest to those who believed in, or wanted to experiment with, the seductive and sensual properties associated with many vegetables, especially leeks and onions. One of the greatest English travellers of the nineteenth century, Sir Richard Burton, described peas, broad beans, radishes, artichokes, lettuce, leeks, and onions as "lascivious meats," confirming the aphrodisiacal properties claimed through the years by earlier writers. In the same vein, gentlemen were told that rubbing the juice of an onion on their bald spots would restore their hair and, of course, enhance their handsome appearance to the ladies.

In addition to all its sterling qualities, the skin of the onion was used to produce colour for dying wool, fleece, spun yarn, flax, or cloth. Hues ranged from bright yellow to a deep brown. Thrifty housewives in the pioneer communities of Canada hoarded the skins until they had enough to make a dye pot for this purpose.

Guide books for farmers and gardeners gave explicit instructions for the successful planting, care, and harvesting of this important household plant. *The Farmer's and Housekeeper's Cyclopaedia* of 1888 tells us:

> Let me say to those who, by reason of repeated failures, have become discouraged and abandoned the growing of onions, that if they will put the following directions in practice they will be astonished at the result. The soil must be clean, rich and light, not a gravelly kind, nor one so dry as to suffer from drought — sandy loam is the best. The ground should be heavily salted, and this well worked in before sowing. The sowing should be done in April, and as early in the month as possible: "delay is dangerous." With a heavy roller, or the feet, the ground should be pressed down quite hard. Weeding should be attended to as soon as you can safely do so. The tops should be left on the bed or field to rot, or to spade or plow in; and onions improve by being grown on the same ground year after year. Plow shallow if you plow at all.

Know Your Onions

It should be noted that if an onion was planted in the centre of a hill of cucumbers, melons, or squash it would deter bugs from feeding on those plants; if planted with roses, the scent of the flowers was much sweeter. Perhaps the final historical bonus was that gold leaf on picture frames could be brightened by rubbing with boiled onion juice and wiping dry.

Despite its long and illustrious history and its virtues of economy, flavour, and versatility, the onion is often overlooked today. However, a large number of the recipes enjoyed by our Canadian ancestors are worth a try. Many of the following appeared for the first time in nineteenth-century Canadian cookbooks such as the *Dominion Cook Book*, 1899, by Anne Clarke, but they have stood the test of time and should make welcome additions to your recipe file:

Spanish Onions Baked
Ingredients: 4 or 5 Spanish onions, butter, salt and water. Salt a saucepanful of boiling water slightly, put the onions into this, leaving the skins on, and let them boil sharply for about an hour. When they are done, take them out, wipe them, and cover each in a piece of brown paper, bake in the oven for two hours. Add butter, pepper and salt to taste, and serve in their skins.

Onions Stuffed
Ingredients: Very large Spanish onions, cold fat pork or bacon, bread crumbs, pepper, salt, mace, 10 spoonfuls of cream or milk, a well beaten egg, butter, juice

of half a lemon, browned flour, milk. Wash and skin very large Spanish onions. Lay in cold water an hour. Parboil in boiling water half an hour. Drain and while hot extract their hearts, taking care not to break the outside layers. Chop the inside thus obtained very fine with a little cold fat pork or bacon. Add bread crumbs, pepper, salt, mace, and wet with a spoonful or two of cream (or milk in default of cream). Bind with a well beaten egg, and work into a smooth paste. Stuff the onions with this; put into a pan with little hot water, and simmer in the oven for an hour, basting with butter melted. Lift them out carefully and arrange the open ends upwards in a vegetable dish. Add to the gravy in the dripping pan the juice of half a lemon, four tablespoons of cream or milk and a little browned flour wet with cold milk. Boil up once, and pour over the onions.

There must be very few casseroles that have not been improved by the addition of one or more onions, and probably everyone has a favourite. Here is a modern one that is easy on the budget:

Onion Bake
Cook 2 cups of sliced onions in 2 tablespoons butter until tender. Do not brown. Spread on bottom of greased baking dish. Meanwhile, boil 6 eggs and peel. Slice over onions. Add 2 cups of Swiss cheese or mild cheddar cheese shredded. Mix 1 can con-

densed cream of chicken soup, 3/4 cup milk, and 1/4 teaspoon pepper in saucepan and stir until smooth. Slowly pour this mixture over the casserole, making sure that it reaches the bottom. Butter four slices of bread, cut off crusts, and cut each into 4 squares. Lay bread over top of the casserole and bake at 350°F for about 30 minutes. You may have to turn on the broiler to brown the bread. Serve hot. Serves about 5 or 6.

And finally, how about a make-ahead salad that is a great favourite in northern Ontario and appears in many modern cookbooks:

Be Prepared Salad
Choose a large bowl and shred a head of lettuce in the bottom. Then add in this order:

1 layer of chopped Spanish onions or green onions
1 layer of celery, chopped fine
1 layer of water chestnuts, sliced (if they are available)
1 layer of frozen peas
1 layer of shredded cheese, either Swiss or mild cheddar

Mix 2 cups of salad dressing with 3 tablespoons of sugar and cover the salad. Leave overnight in a cool place. Will serve about 8 hungry guests.

Toothsome Tomatoes

A world without tomatoes is like a string quartet without violins.
  Laurie Colwin, *Home Cooking*

Through the centuries, the tomato has been considered both a foe and a friend at our tables and has been known by many names, including apple of gold, love apple, and apple from the Moors. The origins of this fruit are shrouded in mystery, for it has been claimed as a native of India, Africa, China, Ecuador, and Peru. It was the Spanish who brought it to Europe, having seen the Peruvians propagating the tomato from a humble red berry and using it as a symbol in decorating their pottery.

It was then considered a decorative plant, and it quickly spread via Morocco into Italy, where, in 1544, Peirandrea Mattioli described it as "a kind of eggplant." He later changed his description to *mala insane*, or unhealthy apple. Within a decade, a written description called it *pomi d'oro*, or apple of gold, so we assume the first variety known to Europeans was yellow.

By the end of the 1500s, both red and yellow varieties were known as curiosities in the gardens of the well-to-do in England, France, Spain, and Italy. The French, always willing to be adventurous when experimenting with new foods, tried cooking the *pomme d'amour*, or love apple (probably so called because of its alleged aphrodisiacal properties). In the meantime, Sir Walter Raleigh presented tomato plants to his queen to be used as decoration in the Royal Gardens.

The word tomato derives from *tomatl* in the native Nahuatl language, and it first appeared in English print in 1604. Despite the French success in cooking it, tomatoes continued to be suspect because they were recognized as a member of the deadly nightshade family, *Solanaceae*. For nearly a century, it was said that only a hapless lover or a potential suicide would toy with a tomato.

The first tomatoes to be cultivated for food in North America were found in dooryard gardens in the eighteenth century. It was Thomas Jefferson who, by growing them in his own garden in 1782, did much to exonerate and legitimize the tomato among his countrymen. Slowly it gained acceptance across the United States, and of course, it was carried into British North America as well. By the middle of the nineteenth century, newspapers and farmers' periodicals began to give advice to the home gardener on the planting, pruning, and training of the plants for maximum quality and quantity.

As the fruit gained acceptance, it began to appear in recipes in printed cookery books. Among the first was "Tomata catsup" in 1792 in *The New Art of Cookery*, written by Richard Briggs and published in England. Briggs was writing about a very current experiment for catsup. A seasoned sauce, often called *liquiamen,* was first prepared by the Romans in 300 B.C. and consisted of a paste made of dried anchovies, pepper, oil, and vinegar. The Chinese developed a seasoned sauce called *ke-tsiap* in 1690, primarily for use on fish and fowl, and it was so popular it spread to the Malay Archipelago, where it was called *kechap*. British seamen brought back samples of the seasoned sauce to English chefs, who tried to duplicate it using the only ingredients they knew, such as cucumbers, mushrooms, and walnuts. Even with these substitutions the sauce became very popular, and Mrs. Sarah Harrison in 1748, in *House-Keeper's Pocket-Book*, cautioned the housewife to "never be without this condiment." Tomatoes were finally tried in catsup recipes about 1790 and were an instant success.

Despite their slow start, tomatoes were coming into their own by the middle of the nineteenth century. Tomato plants were being raised in gardens across North America, and writers like Catharine Parr Traill in *The Canadian Settler's Guide* were encouraging its growth and noting its use as "a dinner vegetable, as a sauce and even as a tart and wine."

The belief persisted that tomatoes should be cooked for hours, and this, combined with the many steps involved in making catsup, turned preparation into a long, time-consuming chore that involved peeling, boiling, stirring, and straining. North American housewives were more than ready for the products that began to appear in 1876 from the factory of Henry Heinz. Heinz Tomato Catsup was billed as "Blessed relief for Mother and the other women in the household!" Heinz went on to produce pickles, relishes, fruit butters, and horseradish and by the end of the century had adopted the slogan "57 Varieties," which has since become world famous.

Toothsome Tomatoes

The cookery books of the last quarter of the nineteenth century began to reflect the versatility of tomatoes as perceived by their authors and the busy housewife. For example, *The Home Cook Book* contains a number of quick and easy recipes using tomatoes, all suitable for modern tastes, including:

Tomato Hash
Butter the dish well; put in a layer of sliced tomatoes, a layer of cold meat, sliced thin; then a layer of bread and butter, and so on until the dish is full, seasoning well with pepper and salt, and beaten eggs poured over the top. Bake brown.

A multitude of tomato-based recipes appeared in the twentieth century, and they were passed from home to home across Canada. Although many of these recipes have been used for close to a century they are still worth trying in your own kitchen.

Tomato Nests
Cut the tops off some peeled tomatoes, remove the inside, drop a raw egg in each, and replace the top as a cover. Bake them until the eggs have set. Serve them very hot with sauce or plain.
Kitchen Ranging by H. Pearl Adam, 1923

Chili Sauce
12 large ripe tomatoes
2 large onions

4 green peppers
2 tablespoons salt
4 tablespoons brown sugar
1 tablespoon cloves
1 tablespoon cinnamon
1 tablespoon allspice
1 teaspoon grated nutmeg
1 pint vinegar

Peel the tomatoes and onions. Cut tomatoes in small pieces and chop the onions and peppers fine. Add the remaining ingredients, heat gradually to boiling point, and cook slowly 2 to 3 hours. Stir frequently. If vinegar is strong, dilute it with water.

L.M.S. Book of Recipes, compiled by A.L. Laird and N.L. Pattinson, 1917

Fried Tomatoes — Green or Ripe
Four tomatoes and one cupful of crumbs, one small onion chopped fine, salt and pepper. If ripe tomatoes are used, choose solid firm ones, not too ripe. Remove skin. If green ones, just beginning to ripen, are used, do not pare, cut a thin paring from the end and divide into slices about one-half inch thick. Prepare the dressing and press it into the tomatoes until all the interstices are filled.

Just for Two, compiled by Amelie Langdon, 1909

Toothsome Tomatoes

Canadians today prefer the red varieties of tomatoes in a multitude of ways — raw, in salads, in sauces, in juices, or in cooked and baked dishes — while in other parts of the world the yellow varieties are still the favourite. New arrivals in Canada bring with them their love of tomato sauces for many of their traditional dishes, and these new condiments jostle for elbow room on the grocers' shelves of the nation along with the old North American favourites all year long. But in the summer, in markets, roadside stands, and our own gardens, the fresh harvest is there to be enjoyed. Search for them and savour the succulence of the season.

The Indispensable Potato

What I say is that if a man really likes potatoes, he must be a pretty decent sort of fellow.
A.A. Milne, *Not That It Matters*

The potato, a favourite Canadian vegetable at any time of the year, has had a special place on our tables for centuries. This lowly tuber has a long and distinguished history, but its strongest ties are perhaps with Ireland, where it was a staple for generations and a factor in shaping the destiny of the Irish people.

A native of the Andes in South America, the white potato (or Irish potato, as it later became known) was first cultivated by the Incas more than four thousand years ago. Pottery decorated with potato motifs has been found in prehistoric burial sites in South America, confirming its existence and its importance to the diet and culture of the period. The Incas called it *papa,* and Spanish explorers carried the potato back to Europe in the sixteenth century. One of them described the potato as "this ground nut which, when boiled becomes as soft as a cooked chestnut but has no thicker skin than a truffle."

This curious new plant spread from Spain to Italy, Flanders, and Germany by the end of the sixteenth century. As well as being recognized as a staple food, herbalists believed the white potato was an aphrodisiac and a cure for rheumatism. During this period the French resisted the potato, as it was rumoured to cause leprosy. Their attitude began to change in the 1700s when the country was plagued by chronic shortages of wheat (and therefore bread), then the staple peasant fare in France. In 1795 Madame Merigot authored and published in Paris *La Cuisinere republicaine*, a remarkable turning point, for not only was this the first cookbook to be published by a woman in France, it was devoted exclusively to potatoes, the once forbidden vegetable.

Meanwhile, Christopher Columbus had also found a tuber called *batata* while exploring the West Indies. Today known as the sweet potato, it was recognized as a source of food and transported back to Spain for propagation. By the fifteenth century it was also established in China and the Philippines.

Legend tells us that it was Sir Walter Raleigh who planted the first white potatoes in Ireland as a guard against famine and who later introduced them into England as well; however, many historians disagree. The potato soon became a staple in Ireland, where it is said that a typical peasant family ate about eight pounds of potatoes per day. By comparison, potatoes had a late start in Scotland, as they were frowned upon by Scottish preachers who believed they were unfit for Christians, as there was no mention of them in the Holy Bible.

Ironically, what began as a precaution against famine was the cause of famine. So reliant were the Irish on potatoes that the country was devastated when the crop failed in 1845. Poor yields over the next four years left one million people dead and another million destitute, with no other choice than emigration. Indeed, the late 1840s saw mass migrations to North America, Australia, and New Zealand. Many Canadians of Irish descent can trace the arrival of their ancestors to those hungry years.

When the Irish arrived in North America, the potato was already here, having reached Boston over a century earlier. It had been grown in New Hampshire and Massachusetts in the 1700s, and some cookbooks of the period carried recipes using it.

Nineteenth-century authors embraced the potato, and even fried potatoes were described as "an admirable way of dressing potatoes" in *Mrs. Hale's New Cookbook* in 1857. Potato chips, often called Saratoga chips, became popular in the mid-1850s as well. Potatoes proved their versatility in many ways. They were boiled, baked, fried, scalloped, and creamed. They were used to make yeast cakes, soups, scones, bread, pancakes, salads, pies, Irish stew, and stuffing for geese. Potato flour was made of cooked, dried, and ground potatoes and was used to thicken soups, sauces, gravies, and puddings. No wonder the lowly vegetable became such an integral part of Canadian cooking traditions. By 1900, North Americans were consuming about two hundred pounds per person per year. By the end of the nineteenth century, potato salad was one of the most popular dishes to serve during the summer months in Canada. Everyone experimented, not only for family meals, but also for community suppers, picnics, pot luck suppers, Queen Victoria's birthday, and other meals of celebration. By the 1920s, combinations of cooked, cold, chopped potatoes, green onions, and chopped hard-boiled eggs were blended with homemade dressing for any, or every, occasion, particularly in the summer months.

In addition to its popularity both hot and cold, the potato was believed to have some medicinal properties. It was indispensable in preventing hardening of the arteries and as an elixir for burns, asthma, and arthritis. Potato remedies were also supposed to cure fever in children, eczema, freckles, frostbite, heartburn, hemorrhoids, inflamed eyes, sciatica, insect stings and bites, and warts. Who would dare to be without potatoes?

Canadians from coast to coast embraced the potato. Prince Edward Island has become famous around the world for its production of potatoes and has also become the home of the Potato Museum and the Potato Blossom Festival located at O'Leary, Prince Edward Island. Try one of the following traditional recipes as a tribute to the humble vegetable that has spanned the centuries and fed the multitudes.

Potato Pie
Scald one quart milk, grate in four large potatoes while the milk is hot, when cold add four eggs well beaten, four ounces butter, spice and sweeten to your taste, lay in paste, bake half an hour.

N.B. A bowl containing two quarts, filled with water, and set into the oven prevents any article from being scorched, such as cakes, pies and the like.

The Cook Not Mad, or Rational Cookery, printed in Canada in 1831, by James Macfarlane of Kingston, Upper Canada. This was one of the first cookery books published here and was a copy of an American book published in Waterdown, New York in 1830.

Potato Soufflé
Quarter of a pound of potatoes, two eggs, chopped parsley.

Bake the potatoes, skin them and put them through a sieve. Separate the yolks and whites of the eggs and beat them, adding to the potatoes first the yolks and then the whites. Add minced parsley, pepper and salt to season, bake about fifteen minutes. Serve straight from the oven.

The Gentle Art of Cookery, 1925

Potato Bread
This began as a traditional Irish recipe known as "Fadge" in counties Derry and Antrim and called "Pratie Bread" in County Down. It is a favourite with Irish Canadians and is delicious fried in bacon fat or heated under the grill and buttered lavishly while still hot.

The Indispensable Potato

1 pound cooked potatoes
4 ounces flour (about)
1/2 teaspoon salt

Put freshly boiled potatoes, while still hot, on the bake board. Bruise with flat-bottomed mug or tin, grasped by the rim and pressed down on each potato in turn until no lumps remain. Over mashed potatoes scatter salt and enough flour to make a pliable paste. The quantity of the flour depends on the quality of the potatoes; soapy potatoes requiring more than floury ones. Knead until elastic enough to roll out. (Too much kneading toughens it). Roll out into a round (fairly thin). Cut into four triangular farls. Bake till brown on both sides, on a hot griddle or fry pan.

Irish Stew

This is a traditional recipe that is still frequently used in both Canada and Ireland today, and is quick and easy for the busy cook.

1 pound neck of mutton (or any lean mutton)
2 pounds potatoes
1/2 pound onions
pepper and salt
hot water

Cut meat into small pieces. Put into pot and cover with hot water. Add salt and boil up. Peel potatoes, cut about one-third of them in slices and add to the pot with the pepper, and stir up. Then lay the rest of the potatoes in large chunks on top and stew for about 2 hours, stirring occasionally. Serve with potato bread.

A Cavalcade of Corn

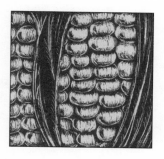

Heap high the farmer's wintry hoard! Heap high the golden corn!
No richer gift has Autumn poured, From out her lavish horn!
John Greenleaf Whittier, "The Corn-Song"

As Canadians gather for the annual corn roasts in the fall and watch the blazing fire while the corn simmers, they join a chain of consumers that stretches back into human history over eighty thousand years.

The first corn plant is believed to have been developed by the natives of Central America from a tall wild grass. Known also as *mais*, *mahiz*, and *maize*, the Pueblo Indians of Central America considered corn a sacred plant, "a gift from the gods" surrounded by legends about its origins, power, and healing qualities. Many of their everyday activities centred around the maize plant as they prepared it for food by popping, parching, boiling, and grinding, or for an alcoholic beverage by inducing fermentation.

When Christopher Columbus arrived in Cuba in 1492, the natives presented him with a gift of corn that he in turn introduced to the Old World upon his return. At first it was grown in Europe as a curiosity and was often called Turkey corn or Turkey wheat. There was some confusion about the origin of corn in Europe, some people believing that it had come from Turkey. It met with mixed reviews, for John Gerard, the renowned English herbalist, describes it at the end of the sixteenth century:

> Turkey wheat doth nourish far lesse than either wheat, rie, barly, or otes. The bread which is made thereof is meanely white, without bran; it is hard and dry as Bisket is, and hath in it no clamminess at all; for which cause it is of hard digestion, and yeeldeth to the body little or no nourishment. We have as yet not certaine proofe or experience concerning the virtues of this kinde of corne; although the barbarous Indians, which know no better, are constrained to make a vertue of necessitie, and thinke it is good food.

This new plant was unlike any other cereal known to the Old World. It was large, and with its naked grains in ears on the side of the stalk instead of on top, it was unique. It was not planted by broadcasting like other grains but in individual hills, preferably with a dead fish in the mound as fertilizer. Some countries immediately accepted maize as a staple of their diet, while other relegated it to the fodder for their livestock.

Maize spread north from Central America, carried on the First Nations' trade routes, so early explorers to Canada found them planting and harvesting corn. Many of the tribes and nations considered it sacred, some calling it their Sacred Mother, one of the Three Sisters (corn, beans, and squash) to be planted together in hills and to be eaten together. Three Sisters Soup is made by boiling the three vegetables together and adding some pork or venison cut into small pieces. This staple food was also used in stews, puddings, breads, and beverages.

Despite its rapid spread to several countries, many travellers in early Canada appeared to treat it as a new plant. John Goddie included corn in his *Description of Some New and Rare Plants Discovered in Canada in the year 1819.*

In 1817 in *Adventures on the Columbia River*, Ross Cox describes corn growing at Fort William, the inland head-quarters of the North West Fur Company (today Old Fort William has been reconstructed, furnished, and opened to the public at Thunder Bay): "A certain amount of agriculture was carried on. There was a garden and extensive fields of Indian corn and potatoes."

In *Daughters of the Country*, W. O'Meara confirms corn as a staple in the diet:

At Fort Williams, for example, where a great many transient voyageurs congregated each summer, the high ranking traders, from agents down to guides, dined very well indeed. They feasted in the great dining hall on bread, salt pork, beef, smoked ham, whitefish, venison, butter, peas, Indian corn puddings, potatoes, tea, brandy and wine — and even milk supplied by the post's two cows. In their tent encampment outside the palisades, the ordinary canoeman had to be content with a mess of boiled Indian corn and tallow.

In the records of these early travellers, trappers, and traders they used the term "Indian corn" to avoid confusion with other grains. In England wheat was called "corn," and in Scotland oats were called "corn."

Although Canadian pioneers always wanted to grow wheat, they often found that it was impossible, and corn soon became a standard crop instead. There are six principal types of corn:

- Pod Corn: probably the original plant from which the others have been developed; it is now grown only as a curiosity.
- Dent corn: usually yellow or white, and with a depression on the crown of the kernel, it is preferred for commercial purposes, e.g., the making of hominy and fodder for animals.
- Flint corn: germinates quickly in cold climates; popular in Canada, New England, and New York state.
- Flour corn: also known as squaw or soft corn, preferred by the First Nations because it can be easily ground or chewed; very popular in Ecuador, Peru, and Bolivia.
- Sweet corn: can be recognized by its wrinkled, translucent seeds because the sugar manufactured by the plant is not converted into starch; used for

human consumption either by roasting, boiling, canning, or freezing.

- Popcorn: a type of flint corn with small, hard kernels that, when heated, cause the moisture in the cell to expand and explode.

Corn has evolved through the centuries through accidental and planned hybridization both by the natives, through trade and travel, and by newcomers. About 1920, corn growers began to realize the vigour and uniformity that could be stimulated by cross and double-cross hybridization, resulting in larger, quicker yields with reduced manpower. This has led to the expansion of hybrid corn, so that today nearly all the North American crop comes from hybrids.

Every part of a corn plant can be used. For example, the stalk is used for wallboard and paper, husks are used for toys and stuffing for mattresses, and cobs are used for corncob pipes and for fuel. The grain is used in over two hundred foods, drugs, and cosmetics. Some of these have been developed through careful experimentation, while others have been lucky accidents.

Cornflakes, the popular breakfast cereal on many Canadian tables, were one of those late nineteenth-century accidents, when American William Kellogg was boiling wheat to make it more digestible and overcooked it. Not daunted, he rolled it out anyway and found that it formed long, thin flakes. He later tried this with corn, and by applying flavouring to the product and energetic advertising to the consumer, he revolutionized North American breakfast tables with his cold cereal, and Kellogg's Corn Flakes was born.

In the twentieth century other products of corn found their way into our pantries, larders, and kitchens. *Canada's Prize Recipes,* compiled by the Canada Starch Co. in 1930, announced:

> Corn, the familiar golden ear which grows in fields by the wayside, and which we have taken for granted so long, is now attracting widespread attention, because of the food products of such high nutritive value that are produced from it.
>
> Corn Syrups and Corn Starches are ranked very high in food value by eminent authorities on nutrition. Their carbohydrate food value being definitely established, they can be considered as a most useful part of any meal and in conjunction with fruits and light proteins form an exceptionally well balanced diet.
>
> Technically, it may mean little to us, yet in fact carbohydrates supply the heat and energy to the body. Without these the human machine cannot go on.

The variety of uses of corn and corn products is endless. The Iroquois prepared corn coffee by parching dried ears on hot embers and scraping the kernels into a container. Boiling water was added and it was again boiled for five minutes. Maple sugar was used as a sweetener.

Both natives and newcomers used the oil of corn grains rubbed into the scalp as a treatment for dandruff. The oil was also used in poultices for boils, burns, and inflammations.

A Cavalcade of Corn

Corn appears in countless Canadian cookbooks through the years. *St. Luke's Cook Book* contains some traditional favourites that appeared not just in Manitoba but right across Canada:

Corn Fritters
Four tablespoons cold corn, one egg, two tablespoons flour, two tablespoons cream, pepper and salt to taste; fry in deep fat.

Cornmeal Pancakes
Three-quarters of a cup of white flour, three cups cornmeal, one egg, one-half cup milk, one-half cup water, two teaspoons baking powder, a little salt; mix together and fry.

Corn Muffins
One and one-half cups flour, one-half cup cornmeal, one cup milk, three teaspoons baking powder, one-half cup sugar, one half teaspoon salt, one-half cup butter, two eggs.

Finally, this recipe has never gone out of favour in Canadian kitchens, and although it has been adapted to modern tastes, it brings two centuries of Canadian tradition with it:

Indian Pudding Served Up with Hot Rum Sauce
4 cups milk
1/3 cup molasses

1/3 cup brown sugar
1/2 cup cornmeal
3/4 teaspoon cinnamon
1/4 teaspoon nutmeg
1 teaspoon salt
4 tablespoons butter

Heat milk and add molasses, sugar, cornmeal, salt, spices, and butter. Cook and stir until mixture thickens. Pour into well-greased baking dish and bake in a slow oven, about 300°F, for about 3 hours. Serve warm, with hot rum sauce.

Hot Rum Sauce
4 tablespoons butter
1 cup brown sugar
1 tablespoons flour
1 cup water
1/4 cup rum (or rum flavouring)

Brown butter, sugar, and flour, and add water slowly, stirring as it thickens. Remove from heat, add rum, and beat until smooth. Serve immediately.

Canadians have eaten it, drunk it, slept on it, woven it into clothing, burned it for heat, and used it in a multitude of other ways, but we have never lost our fascination with corn. May it continue to be an important part of our everyday life for the next eighty thousand years.

Peter, Peter, Pumpkin-Eater

I light the prairie cornfields Orange and tawny gold clusters And I am called pumpkins.
  Carl Sandburg, "Theme in Yellow"

Squash is the name we often use in Canada to include a wide variety of vegetables that grow throughout the western hemisphere. They are native to the Americas and were known and grown by the First Nations long before the arrival of explorers from other countries. Evidence of squash dating from 7,000 to 5,500 B.C. has been found at the Ocampa Caves in Mexico, and from there it would have travelled north. In the eastern United States, two-thousand-year-old burial mounds have yielded up similar evidence.

Among many First Nations, squash, beans, and corn were known as the Three Sisters. They were grown together, the corn standing tall and straight, the beans climbing the corn stalks, and the squash spreading out to control the weeds. When they were harvested, they were often eaten together to complement one another.

Early European explorers searching for the treasures of the Indies found instead the culinary treasures of the Americas, including squash. Although usually associated with North American cooking, squash was also carried to other parts of the world. In Great Britain, the common name for squash is vegetable marrow.

There are three well-known categories of squash: summer varieties such as the yellow crookneck and zucchini; autumn and winter squash such as Hubbard, butternut, and acorn; and pumpkins, which are in a category by themselves. Pumpkins are differentiated from squash by having rougher, woodier, squarish stems; squash stems by contrast are rounder and tenderer. A newcomer to the squash family is the spaghetti squash or vegetable spaghetti — its stringy flesh is often served with pasta sauces. Another new arrival from Latin America is the *calabaza,* a very large squash often sold in large wedges. It is very versatile and can be used in any recipe that calls for pumpkin. Sweet potato squash, meanwhile, has a mottled dark green and cream-coloured skin and, as the name suggests, a sweet, mellow flavour.

The appearance of freshly harvested winter squash at stores, markets, and roadside stands is a sure sign that autumn has arrived. Because squash is more readily available and less expensive in the fall than at any other time of the year, it is the perfect opportunity to experiment with this versatile vegetable. It can be enjoyed in a variety of different ways: as a dish in its own right or in soups, breads, puddings, and pies. It can also be decorative: scooped out and used to serve soup or arranged in groups for autumn centerpieces. There is no shortage of ways you can put squash, with its long and honourable history, on your table, so perk up fall menus with these savoury recipes.

Hearty Pumpkin Soup
1 large onion, finely chopped
2 tablespoons butter
3 cups chicken broth (either homemade or canned)
1 large potato, peeled and diced
2 medium carrots, peeled and diced
1 16-ounce can pumpkin or 2 cups fresh puréed pumpkin
2 stalks celery, sliced
1/2 pint whipping cream

Using a large saucepan on medium heat, sauté chopped onion in hot butter. Add chicken broth and heat. Add vegetables and cook over low heat until vegetables are tender (about 12 to 15 minutes). Add pumpkin and a little salt and pepper to taste. Heat just to boiling, cover, and reduce heat to simmer for at least 5 minutes. Stir in cream and heat through. Serve in bowls, from a soup tureen, or from a fresh, seeded pumpkin. Serves about 6. If you have other favourite vegetables you want to add to this soup, go ahead and experiment — they will also stretch the recipe to more servings.

Honey and Hazelnut Filling
2 1-pound acorn squash, cut in half lengthwise and seeded
1/4 cup hazelnuts with skins removed

3 tablespoons unsalted butter
4 teaspoons honey

Bake squash for about 45 minutes at 350°F until tender. Meanwhile, toast hazelnuts separately for about 10 minutes until they begin to smell fragrant. Chop well. Melt butter and divide among the squash cavities, add hazelnuts and honey evenly to each. Sprinkle with salt to taste and return to the oven for about 12 minutes or until the mixture in the cavity begins to bubble. Makes 4 generous servings. Serve hot.

Squash Casserole
6 cups cooked squash
4 tablespoons butter
4 tablespoons maple syrup
1/4 teaspoon cinnamon
1/4 teaspoon nutmeg
1 teaspoon salt
dash pepper

Peel squash, remove seeds, cut into pieces, and steam or boil until soft. Drain carefully and mash. Add other ingredients and mix well. Spoon into a greased casserole dish to serve or store in the refrigerator to reheat and serve later. Serves 8. This is an excellent make-ahead dish if you know you will be pressed for time.

Squash Pie
3/4 cup sugar
1 tablespoon all-purpose flour
1/2 teaspoon salt
1/4 teaspoon ground ginger
1 1/2 teaspoons crushed aniseed
3/4 teaspoon lemon juice
3 eggs
1 1/2 cups winter squash, cooked and mashed
1 cup milk
pastry for 1-crust 9-inch pie

Combine the first six ingredients in a mixing bowl. Beat in eggs. Stir in squash and milk. Turn into 9-inch pie plate lined with pastry. Bake in preheated 400°F oven for 40 to 50 minutes or until tester comes out clean. Cool before serving. Serves 6 to 8. Squash pie can be served plain or with whipped cream or vanilla ice cream.

Roasted Seeds
seeds from squash or pumpkin
3 tablespoons butter
salt, garlic salt, or seasoning salt

Remove seeds from squash or pumpkin and clean by removing all excess fibres. Rinse and lay on a paper towel to dry. Melt butter in shallow pan. Stir in seeds, sprinkle with your favourite salt, and bake at 300°F until brown and crisp. Stir once or twice while toasting.

Squash Blossoms
1 1/2 cups squash blossom buds
1 tablespoon butter
salt and pepper

Wash and dry blossom buds. Heat butter in frying pan or chafing dish, add blossoms, and turn gently. Most of them will burst into blossom as they cook. Watch the heat and do not let them brown. Sprinkle with salt and pepper and serve immediately.

Baked Squash
Cut an acorn squash in half and scoop out seeds and fibres. Brush with melted butter and sprinkle with brown sugar and a pinch of salt. Bake at 350°F for 1 hour or until tender. There are numerous variations on this recipe that call for different fillings: try maple syrup instead of brown sugar; bacon crisply fried and combined with maple syrup; or a stuffing made of onions, bread crumbs, and seasonings (such as you would make for fowl), or Honey and Hazelnut Filling.

Zucchini Bread
2 eggs
1/2 cup oil
1 cup sugar
1 cup zucchini, washed, unpeeled, grated
1 teaspoon vanilla
2 cups flour
1 teaspoon baking powder
1 teaspoon baking soda
1/2 teaspoon salt

Beat eggs well, add oil, sugar, zucchini, and vanilla. Mix remaining five ingredients in separate bowl and add to zucchini mixture. Stir well. Pour into greased loaf pan. Bake in 350°F oven 50 to 60 minutes. Let stand 5 to 10 minutes, then turn out on rack to cool. Wrap well. Store in a cool place.

Of Cabbages and Kings

The cabbage surpasses all other vegetables. If, at a banquet, you wish to dine a lot and enjoy your dinner, then eat as much cabbage as you wish, seasoned with vinegar, before dinner, and likewise after dinner eat some half-dozen leaves. It will make you feel as if you had not eaten, and you can drink as much as you like.

Cato (Marcus Porcius), Roman politician and general.

Centuries ago wild cabbages (also known as sea cabbages) found near the east coast of England and continental Europe were cultivated as an important food source and also as medicine. For example, Roman physicians used the cabbage as a cure for headache, colic, deafness, drunkenness, insomnia, and internal ulcers. In addition, cabbage leaves dipped in hot water and applied to wounds and abscesses brought "remarkable results."

It was Captain James Cook on the voyage of the *Endeavour*, from 1768 to 1771, who was credited with recording the incredible properties of cabbage when made into sauerkraut for the prevention of scurvy. He reported in the *Journals of Captain James Cook On His Voyages of Discovery Volume 1* in July of 1771:

I am to acquaint you that Sour Kroutt together with the many other Antiscorbutics my Lord Commrs. of the Admiralty were pleased to order to be put on board did so effectually preserve the People from a Scorbutic Taint that no one dangerous case happened in that disorder during the Whole Voyage…

The early settlers of British North America found cabbage to be a practical vegetable to plant in the gardens and fields carved out of virgin forest, for it grows best in mild to cool climates and will tolerate frost. In the uncertain Canadian climate this was an important attribute.

The Farmer's and Housekeeper's Cyclopedia also stressed that where space was at a premium, cabbages could be started indoors from seed and then placed between rows of potatoes and sweet corn that would shade the cabbages until they were established, and when the potatoes and corn were harvested the cabbages could mature on the same ground.

Although sauerkraut on board ship was established among seamen by the eighteenth century, it was the Pennsylvania German settlers who brought this food tradition to Canadian communities:

Sauerkraut
10 pounds of white cabbage
1/4 pound salt

Free the tight, fresh cabbages from their outer leaves and shred. Put alternate layers of cabbage and salt into a clean stoneware vessel. Compress each layer with a wooden plunger until the juice stands above the cabbage. Put a couple of cabbage leaves on top, and then a linen cloth which has been boiled in water. The cabbage is then weighted with a piece of clean wood (approximately the same diameter as the pot) and a stone. Tie another piece of cloth across the opening of the container, which should then be stored in a cool place. The fermentation takes about 4 to 6 weeks, during which time cloth, stone and wood should be rinsed every 10 to 14 days. Layers of grape leaves or apples can be put in with the cabbage. If, at any time during the fermentation, the juice does not stand above the cabbage, salted water should be added. Always use a clean wooden spoon to remove sauerkraut from its container. As well as eating it raw, it can be cooked with bacon and onions, made into casseroles with potatoes, meat and cheese, or into soup by combining it with beef bouillon.

Irish settlers were also fond of cabbage, and it was for this reason that Cabbagetown in Toronto was named. Evidently the Irish settlers in the area used every available inch of space around their homes to grow cabbages for their tables and for sale, the name stuck, and the legend lives on.

Boiling appears to have been the most popular way for our ancestors to prepare cabbage, although a few more elaborate recipes appear, such as the following from *A Practical Cook* by Ann Miller, published in 1845:

Cabbage And Rice

Shred a large white cabbage, or whatever size you require. Weigh it and take the same weight in rice. In a deepish, fireproof casserole dish (suitable for the top of the stove) place a layer of rice, season it and add a few little pats of butter to the surface. Add a layer of cabbage, season and interlard with bits of butter. Repeat the layers according to the quantity wanted. Add enough water to cover, about half a pint for a large cabbage. Season with salt, pepper and a little mace. Bring to a boil and then simmer very gently covered on top of the stove until both rice and cabbage are tender, about 30 minutes. For knowing this, it is better to make the last layer of rice, as this is less good when overcooked. If the water evaporates too much, add a little more, but it should be boiling and lightly seasoned.

Scottish settlers who came to Canada considered cabbage a favourite and pickled it in barrels (much like sauerkraut) for use in broth, soups, and stews and for making that great favourite "rumbledethumps," which was often eaten as a main course, meatless dish — the unusual name means "mixed together."

Rumbledethumps
4 cups cooked cabbage
4 cups cooked potatoes

2 tablespoons butter
4 tablespoons grated cheddar cheese
1 medium onion, chopped
chopped chives

Melt the butter in a large saucepan, add the onion, and cook gently for about 5 minutes. Add potatoes, cabbage, and chives and mix well. Season with salt and pepper. Grease a large pie plate or shallow casserole dish and place all the ingredients in it. Cover with the grated cheese (add more cheese if you are a cheese lover) and brown in the oven. Serve hot. Will serve about 6 to 8.

In the early twentieth century, a family get-together, church supper, or community meal would not be complete without a cabbage salad of some type. It might range from shredded cabbage, carrots, and onions mixed with salad dressing to a more elaborate moulded jellied salad such as the one from *Mrs. Flynn's Cookbook*:

Moulded Salad
1 cup chopped cabbage
1 cup chopped celery
1 cup chopped tart apples
1 cup chopped walnuts
1 package lemon jelly powder
1 pint boiling water

Dissolve lemon jelly powder in boiling water and when cool, but not set, add the above ingredients. Pour in a mould and allow to stand until set. When wanted, turn out and pour salad dressing over it. This is especially nice with cold fowl and meat.

Although cabbage was sometimes maligned by the elite as common and unsophisticated, it's now being acknowledged as one of the healthiest vegetables you can eat. We shouldn't be surprised, therefore, to see cabbage regain its place as one of the monarchs of the vegetable kingdom as more and more people adopt an interest in healthy eating. Next time you go grocery shopping, buy a cabbage or two — and let this recipe, a favourite with many cultural groups across Canada, introduce you to the delicious versatility of this inexpensive vegetable:

Cabbage Rolls
1 large cabbage
1 1/2 pounds ground beef
1 egg
1/4 cup uncooked rice
1/4 cup water
1 large grated onion
juice of 1 lemon
1/2 cup brown sugar
1 can of tomatoes (28 ounces)
salt and pepper

Cut the heart out of the cabbage and place in enough boiling water to cover. Boil for 5 minutes, separate the leaves, and drain well. Mix the beef with the eggs, rice, water, half the onion, and season with salt and pepper. Place a heaping tablespoon of the mixture on each cabbage leaf, fold over opposite sides, and roll up carefully. If necessary, secure the rolls with toothpicks. Place the rolls in a heavy pot, cover with the tomatoes, sugar, water, the rest of the grated onion, and lemon juice. Cook for 2 hours in a tightly covered pot on top of the stove, then remove the cover and place in a 350°F oven for 1 hour. Depending on your pot, you may have to move to a casserole dish. This will make between 12 and 20 cabbage rolls, depending on the size of the cabbage and the size of the rolls.

Pear Essentials

The Canon sighed, but rousing cried, I answer to thy call,
And a Warden pie's a dainty dish to mortify withal.
  Thomas Ingoldsby, *The Ingoldsby Legends*

"Always a bridesmaid, never a bride" could easily describe many Canadians' attitude to the pear. Often mentioned with the universally beloved apple, the pear always seems to come second in our affections. Next to the apple, it is cultivated more extensively than any other fruit in all parts of the world except tropical and sub-tropical lands, and yet it has never quite captured our hearts in exactly the same way.

Historical records show us that the pear probably originated in China and has been cultivated since at least 2000 B.C. The Romans discovered or developed thirty-eight varieties of pear that were either eaten raw or preserved whole by immersing them, stems and all, in honey. As the Romans conquered Europe they took the fruit trees, vines, and spices that were all part of their food culture with them. The warden pears referred to in these recipes grew in England in medieval times. They were shaped like an acorn squash, probably bright green with black skin bruises. When picked they were probably very hard and tasted like winter pears and quince. This recipe from *The Good Huswife's Jewell* by Thomas Dawson in the sixteenth century told how to conserve them:

Pears in Sirrope
Take your wardens and put them into a great Earthen pot and cover them close, set them in an Oven when you have set in your white bread and when you have drawne your white bread, and your pot and that they be so colde as you may handle them then pill the thin skinne from over a pewter dish that you may save all the sirrope that falleth from them; put to them a quarte of the same sirrope and a pinte of Rosewater and boile them together with a fewe Cloves and Sinnamon and when it is reasonable thick and cold put your wardens and sirrope into a Galley pot and see alwaies that the sirrope bee above the wardens or any other thing that you conserve.

By the seventeenth century, recipes were easier to understand, and a lot more flavourful, if we compare this one from *The Family Dictionary* of 1695:

Pears, to Stew
Take the greatest Wardens, bake them in an oven with Household Bread, putting in a pint of Strong Ale or Beer; when Baked take them from the Liquor; take half a pint of it, half a pint of Red Port and four ounces of Sugar; put them into the Stew-pan, with two Cloves slit, and a little Cream; cover

198

them close, and let them stew till they are very Red; turn them now and then; when they are enough, put them into a dish you intend to serve them in at Table and strew double refined loaf sugar on them.

It would appear that pears were either eaten raw or served as a dessert until the seventeenth and eighteenth centuries, when French hygienists began to recommend eating fruit at the beginning of a meal, thus introducing the idea of pear wedges as *hors d'oeuvres* or combined with other fruit in a cocktail, which, of course, is still popular today.

It was also found that a pleasing beverage called perry, both still and sparkling, could be made from pear juice, in the same way as apple cider. Perry became a favourite, at home, to take to the fields, and at formal feasts and banquets. In 1676 a much-travelled English gentleman and connoisseur of wine wrote a book on wines extracted from fruits in Britain called *Vinetum Brittanicum* that says "the richest wine this world affords is made from the grape, but for the English climate perry and cider are better."

It is believed that the pear was brought to North America by several newcomers, almost simultaneously: Jesuit missionaries, English settlers in Massachusetts, the Dutch in New Amsterdam to the eastern seaboard in the seventeenth century, and Spanish missionaries in the west.

In Canada, the pear was first mentioned in a catalogue by Charles Barnhart called the *Catalogue of Fruit and Ornamental Trees and shrubs, etc.*, published in 1837. In North America the best known and most common, thanks to Enoch Bartlett of Dorchester, Massachusetts, was the Bartlett.

Today it still accounts for three quarters of all pear production on this continent. In other parts of the world, it is called the William, or William's Bon Chrétien, because legend has it that the fruit was brought to France in the fifteenth century by St. Francis of Paola (bon Chrétien means "good Christian" in French) and then was propagated on the continent by a horticulturist named William.

In colonial Canada, pears were presented in a number of ways in nineteenth-century cookery books, as the two recipes that follow will attest:

Potatoes and Pears
Wash and peel the potatoes, cut them in pieces; peel, core, and cut in quarters in the same quantity of pears; parboil the potatoes in water, with some salt. Partly cook the pears with water, butter, and a little vinegar. Strain the potatoes, add the pears, stir them often, and let them cook until quite tender. Serve them hot.

Pear Ice
Take finely flavoured pears, grate them fine and make them very sweet, and freeze them. They are very delicious and make a fine dessert.

Today there are about fifteen thousand species of the pear, all descended from the same common pear (*pyrus com-*

munis) or the Chinese pear (*pyrus sinensis*) of ancient times, so it has been a prolific fruit through the centuries. Perhaps the reason that pears have never quite achieved the popularity of apples in Canada is because they are not as easily stored. Pears are much more prone to tree and storm damage and have a relatively short shelf life. To be at their best they must be picked before they ripen on the tree, or else they will become mealy. In our uncertain Canadian climate, this is an added challenge to the grower.

Juicy, sweet dessert pears should be eaten raw or used in salads, while cooking pears can be poached, stewed, or bottled using these simple, easy to prepare recipes:

Good Fruit Salad
8 oranges
juice of 1 lemon
1 grapefruit
2 or 3 mandarins or tangerines
2 pears
2 apples
3 bananas
1 bunch green grapes
sugar to taste
maraschino cherries (optional)
Pistachio nuts (optional)

Squeeze the juice of 4 of the oranges and add to the lemon juice in a large bowl. Cut up the fruit and leave it in the juice to prevent browning. Peel the other 4 oranges and free the segments from the skin, repeat with the grapefruit and mandarins or tangerines. Peel and core the pears and cut into delicate wedges. Peel the apples, cut fairly thick sections, and then cut in half. Cut the bananas into small circles, cut the grapes in half (remove seeds, if any). Sprinkle sugar over fruit if desired to sweeten. Decorate with a few maraschino cherries and toss. If you are using Pistachio nuts, blanch and skin and add to the top of the bowl. Chill. Serves 8 to 10.

The recipe for Poires Belle-Hélène is attributed to August Escoffier "the king of chefs and the chef of kings." Here is a simple recipe for the famous dish:

Pears Hélène
Peel some ripe pears and poach in a syrup of sugar and water, flavoured with vanilla. Let them cool in the syrup. Serve in individual dishes on a bed of vanilla ice cream with a generous serving of chocolate sauce on top.

To turn Pears Hélène into Pears Melba, substitute a purée of sweetened raspberries for the chocolate sauce.

Baked Pears
Peel and core some pears, cut them into halves, and lay them in a pie plate; fill the centre of each pear with a nut of fresh butter, sprinkle sugar freely over

them, and bake in a hot oven, about 400°F. Serve hot or cold with cream, ice cream, or whipped cream.

Finally, if you own a pear tree, or know someone who does, here is way to impress your loved ones, teacher, boss, landlord, or anyone else that you want to impress — this suggestion comes to us from the *Charleston Courier* of 1868:

> I have just seen a very pretty and fanciful idea developed on pears and apples, in the orchard of a friend at West Roxbury, Massachusetts. As you ramble among trees, you are ever and anon saluted by an inscription on the fruit, done, as it were, by the hand of Nature herself. Here you meet with the familiar name of Mary or Alice or a date (1868) in brief, everything that may suggest itself to your taste or fancy; and all done in the skin of the fruit, without abrasion or any foreign impression. The discovery was made by Hon. Arthur W. Austin, of West Roxbury in 1851. He observed, during the former year, that apples did not redden in that part of the fruit where a leaf happened to lie upon it. In 1852, he cut letters from newspapers, and when the apples were yet green, he pasted them upon the fruit with gum tragacanth. The fruit would then redden to perfection, the letters were removed, and they would appear permanently outlined in green. So, again, when he pasted on the apple a paper in which the letters were

cut out, the parts covered by the paper would be green, and the letters would appear distinctly turned in red, the green surrounding them. The experiment is a very pretty one, and produces a happy effect. Let our fruit growers try it.

Yes, indeed, fruit growers, here is a newly revived historic way of saluting your public. Watch for those personalized pears coming to a community near you soon!

An Apple a Day

Stay me with flagons, comfort me with apples: for I am sick of love.
Ecclesiastes XII, 5

Apples have been a favourite cooking fruit for thousands of years. A member of the rose family, the apple is a native of southeastern Europe and southwestern Asia and probably originated in the area immediately south of the Caucasus. Apples were cultivated four thousand years ago in Egypt, and in Rome, Pliny the Elder described thirty-six varieties that had developed by the first century A.D. As early as the ninth century, a Christian doctor in Baghdad, Ububchaym de Baldach, recommended the medical properties of apples in his writings:

> Cold in the second degree, and moist in the first, the sharp apple is best when it has a high water content. Because of their cold moist nature these apples relieve an overheated liver. Care should be taken lest they harm the chest and voice. The remedy is to eat them with "chaloe" sweetened with honey.

The Romans were also credited with carrying apples into Europe and Britain, where hundreds of varieties developed.

Nothing More Comforting

The First Nations had well-developed agricultural systems when the early explorers arrived in Canada. Both Cartier and Champlain observed that many of the natives supplemented their cultivated vegetables and grains with wild cane and vine fruits as well as wild apples, cherries, and walnuts. The United Empire Loyalists who flooded into British North America at the end of the American Revolution also brought seeds, cuttings, and recipes as well as the skills and knowledge needed to develop flourishing orchards. The success of some of the resulting orchards was expressed very clearly by Timothy Ruggles, a United Empire Loyalist who settled in Wilmont Township in Nova Scotia, writing to a friend in New York in 1783:

> Your fruit trees, when compared by these here — I mean apple — are hardly worth noticing. About 10 days ago I had a present of well toward a bushel of as fine, fair, sound, high-flavoured apples, as you ever saw at New York in the month of January. Colonel Allen of Jersey told me he had drunk the best Cyder here he has ever drunk in his life ...

Another Loyalist, John McIntosh, settled near Dundela in Dundas County (in present-day Ontario) in 1796 and found about twenty young apple trees already growing on his land. He transplanted them, and his son Allen, who learned to graft, subsequently developed the famous McIntosh Red apple. Many Canadians still consider this the finest apple on the market for either eating or cooking.

An Apple a Day

On March 22, 1789, Captain William Booth, a Royal Engineer posted at Shelburne, Nova Scotia, entered in his diary:

> Having had a goose brought to me by Mrs. Bolderness I requested her to do me the honour of partaking of it with two of her children. They dined with me to-day. Gave Veal soup Cranberry Tart with apples nuts and some sweetmeats.

To be able to serve apples to his guests in March, Captain Booth must have succeeded in using one of the ingenious methods that were recommended for keeping fruit fresh over the winter season. These included wrapping in paper, packing in bran, sand, or sawdust, candying in sugar, or rubbing with chalk and dipping in a mixture of beeswax, tallow, and rosin and storing in a cool, dry place.

A far more common, and successful, method was to pare, core, and cut apples into slices so that they could be hung on strings or laid on racks to dry.

Catharine Parr Traill, in *The Canadian Settler's Guide,* describes an apple paring bee in preparation for the drying of apples:

> Bushels and bushels of apples are pared, cored and strung on Dutch thread, by the young men and maidens, and the walls of the kitchen festooned round with apples, where they hung till dry and shrivelled.

They should be dipped into boiling water as they are hung up; this preserves the colour.

In 1872, when *Fruits and Fruit Trees of North America* was published, there were almost one thousand apple trees of North American origin listed — eighty-four of these varieties were being grown in Ontario alone. Canada's fresh fruit exports (largely Ontario apples) subsequently increased from $30,000 in 1868 to $364,000 ten years later. British and European settlers made clear distinctions between cooking and dessert apples. Cooking apples were usually large, green, and acidic, while dessert apples were small, dark, sweet, and fragrant. Cooking apples exceeded all other fruits for use in a variety of recipes — everything from pies, sauces, omelettes, puddings, charlottes, and fools to cobblers, compotes, butter, dumplings, relishes, puffs, tarts, turnovers, fritters, hedgehogs, and soufflés.

Although many old apple varieties, such as Parry White and Sour Bough, have vanished from our fruit stands and markets, Canadians continue their love affair with apples and the number of ways that they can be used in recipes have changed very little over the years. Among the Pennsylvania Germans who settled in Canada in the early nineteenth century, recipes have remained the same for generations, including:

Snitz-Pie
2 cups dried apples (snitz)
1 1/2 cups water
3/4 cups sugar

1/2 teaspoons cinnamon
pastry for a two-crust pie

Soak dried apples for eight hours in water. Cook in
the same water until soft, and mush or put through a
colander. Add sugar and cinnamon. In the meantime
prepare pastry-lined pie plate. Turn apple mixture into
it, dot with butter, and cover with top crust or lattice
strips of pastry. Bake in a quick oven (about 425°F for
10 minutes) and then reduce to a medium oven
(about 350°F for 35 minutes).

In the fall you will have a wide selection of apples to
choose from as the harvest from Canadian orchards reaches
roadside stands, stores, and markets across the country. Why
not try a new variety this autumn and cook up some traditional apple treats for your family and friends?

Apple Hedgehog
6 cooking apples
3/4 cup sugar
whipped cream or custard
almonds cut into slivers

Peel, core, and slice apples into a saucepan. Add sugar
and boil until the mixture drops from a spoon. Put in
a mould, bowl, or individual dishes and cool thoroughly. Before serving, stick strips of blanched
almonds all over it (to look like the quills on a hedge-

hog) and decorate with custard or whipped cream around the edges.

Apple Charlotte
8 cooking apples, peeled, cored, and cut in quarters
1 cup sugar
2 tablespoons butter, and some melted butter
several slices of stale bread
1 slice lemon rind

Cut the crusts off stale bread, dip slices in melted butter, and line the bottom and sides of a mould, a deep pie dish, or a casserole. Stew the peeled, cored, and quartered apples with one cup of water, the sugar, and the lemon rind. When apples are soft, stir in the butter. Pour into the bread–lined mould or casserole and cover with a layer of stale bread dipped in melted butter. Sprinkle with sugar. Bake in a moderate oven, 350°F, until the top layer of bread is golden brown. Serve warm with pouring or whipped cream.

Apple Dowdy
Peel and quarter firm, tart apples and place them in a deep earthenware or ovenproof dish. Fill the dish and then sprinkle with brown sugar, depending on the size of the dish and the tartness of the apples. Sprinkle lightly with salt, nutmeg, and cinnamon. Cut some slivers of butter over the top and add about 1/2 cup of warm water.

Crust:
1 cup flour
2 teaspoons baking powder
2 tablespoons butter
1/4 teaspoon salt
1/2 cup milk

Mix and roll out to about 3/4-inch thickness to cover your dish. Cut a design in the centre for the steam to escape and place it over the apples, pinching to edge of the dish. Bake in slow oven, not higher then 300°F, for about three hours. Serve with pouring cream, or even better, whipped cream flavoured with a little nutmeg.

Apple Stuffing
1 cup celery, diced
2 cooking onions, chopped
2 cups apples, diced
4 tablespoons butter
1 tablespoon lemon juice
1/2 teaspoon dry mint or 1 teaspoon fresh mint, chopped

Sauté the vegetables in butter. Sprinkle the diced apples with lemon juice. Mix all ingredients. Can be used with roast pork, duck, goose, or fish. For variation, substitute 1/4 teaspoon each of basil, marjoram, and thyme for the mint.

Rewards of the Harvest

Come, ye thankful people, come, Raise the song of harvest-home,
All is safely gathered in, Ere the winter storm begins.
  George Job Elvey, *The Hymnary*

As the days grow shorter and our calendars remind us that autumn has arrived again, we begin to look at our gardens and our fields with speculative eyes, just as Canadians have been doing for generations. Our climate has always dictated the harvesting of fields and gardens as insurance against the long winter ahead. The harvest is just the first step, for then comes the storing, preserving, and drying of the yield so that it can be used for planting next year, for food, or for decorative purposes. As a result, the autumn season, more than any other, is filled with a hectic round of activity to beat the weather and to devise new and easier ways of keeping the fruit, vegetables, roots, seeds, grains, and grasses for the future.

Also at this time of the year, there is a blending of traditions that have survived from both our Native and pioneer ancestors. For example, Indian corn will soon begin to appear on front doors across the country, the modern version of the ears of corn that would have been tied to the entrance of a Native home, representing the six tribes of the Iroquois nation — the Seneca, Cayuga, Mohawk, Oneida, Onondaga, and Tuscarora — and acknowledging the blessing of a good harvest and the hope of bringing good fortune until the next year.

Many settlers from the British Isles brought with them memories of corn dollies plaited from several stalks and heads of wheat that were cut from the last sheaf of wheat at harvest time. Wheat was called corn in Britain, thus the name. These were hung in the barn or home (sometimes in the kitchen) until the next year to bring good fortune and bountiful crops. Although the making of corn dollies does not appear to have survived the voyage across the Atlantic with those first settlers, they are now enjoying a revival and can be found in modern homes and offices to bring good luck to the occupants.

There are many examples of pioneer families in Canada keeping some of their first harvest in the new land to commemorate the richness of Canadian soil. It was this sense of accomplishment, not to mention memories of harvest festivals in Europe, that brought harvest activities into the forefront in many communities in the nineteenth century. These were community celebrations, often tied to a local fair and usually culminating in religious services in which the best of the harvest — fruits, flowers, vegetables, and seeds — were used as decoration. In many communities, churches, and museum villages across Canada these "Harvest Home" services are still celebrated today.

Fall fairs are still popular, with some of the older fairs moving to larger and more convenient grounds to accommodate the increased crowds. These trends keep alive the Canadian traditions of harvesting, preserving, and selling or sharing the produce. Such occasions also offer the opportunity to patronize country markets and roadside stands to make up for the limitations of our own gardens and our local stores. Some specialized items are only available in the fall at the time they are harvested, and we encourage you to try some of the following:

Sunflowers

Sunflowers are believed to be native to the Americas and were reported as early as 1615 by Champlain when he visited the Huron Nation near Georgian Bay. Every part of the plant is useful: the oil for cooking, the dried leaf for tobacco, and the stalk for producing a silken fibre. Have you ever tried the seeds?

Roasted Sunflower Seeds
3 tablespoons oil
1/2 pound sunflower seeds

In a shallow bowl or pan that is ovenproof, combine the oil and the sunflower seeds. Toss so that the seeds are completely covered in oil. Place in a 350°F oven for about 20 minutes. Stir several times. Add a sprinkle of salt if desired. When cool, store in a covered container in the refrigerator. If you find this combination too bland for your taste, combine 3 tablespoons of soy sauce with the oil and increase the sunflower seeds to 1 pound.

Wild Rice

Wild rice is a very tall, aquatic grass that grows naturally in many parts of Canada and the upper midwestern United States. The First Nations, particularly the Ojibwe (Ojibway, Ojibwa) Nation, believed that it was provided by the Great Spirit to keep them fit and strong. Each year in September at the time of the "rice moon" they move to camps close to the water and the ripening rice, just as they have done for generations. It is harvested by the women: working in pairs, moving among the stalks in a canoe, bending the stalks over, and pounding them until the seeds fall into the canoe. This crop has been a staple in the diet of the First Nations for centuries, and today wild rice has become important to their economy. It is harvested in large quantities and made available to consumers from selected outlets. With the husk removed, the rice is preserved by drying and parching; then it can be stored until ready to be used. Boiled in salt, water, and lard, wild rice has become popular as an accompaniment to casseroles and hot dishes, as a stuffing for fowl, and as an addition to pancakes, salads, biscuits, breads, and soups. Gourmets around the world not only treasure wild rice for its unique, nutty flavour, but also prize the meat of waterfowl or birds that have fed on it, such as bustards, ducks, swans, and geese, as they believe "they are particularly tender, rich, juicy and delicate."

Caraway Seeds

Caraway has been cultivated since the twelfth century as a medicinal plant, but in North America it has been valued for its culinary uses as well. *The Cook Not Mad* gives us a recipe for using caraway seeds:

> *Nice Cookies that will keep good three months*
> Nine cups of flour, three and a half of butter, five of sugar, large coffee cup of water, with a heaping teaspoonful of pearlash (substitute baking soda) dissolved in it; rub your butter and sugar into the flour, great spoonful of caraway.

This recipe does not give directions, but I have learned from experience that it should be mixed well, small amounts rolled into a ball and flattened very thin on a buttered cookie sheet with a fork, and baked in a moderate oven of 350°F for about 10 minutes or until golden brown. The flavour of the caraway is unmistakable in them.

The results of the harvest did not always find their way onto the table or into the seeders the following year, for our ancestors found seeds and grains had a beauty that could be exhibited in shadow boxes and other ornamental ways. *Cassell's Household Guide*, published in the late nineteenth century, gives some suggestions for decorative uses:

Seed Boxes

It is possible to make from ordinary seeds glove-boxes, bezique boxes [card boxes], and boxes for charitable contributions, that are very ornamental. Commence with the sides. Draw the pattern first in ink. Cover one side of the box with thick glue. Drop on the seeds so as to form patterns. The pattern may be black, and the ground yellow, or two or three colours and shades may be introduced. The common seeds that we give our birds — canary, rape, and maw seed — look very well. Any gardener will help the amateur to a number of pretty seeds for the purpose. They must be very small.

There are many other ways of incorporating the harvest into everyday foods. Homemade bread, for example, can be improved and made moister and more nutritious by replacing up to one-eighth of the flour (particularly in dark breads) with ground sesame or sunflower seeds. Other substitutions can be seed or nut butter, for example peanut butter, or leftover cooked cereal.

Perhaps it's no surprise that seeds were such an important component of the ancestral kitchen. After trying some recipes and using seeds for decorative accents, you'll soon discover they have an equally important place in the modern household as well.

High on the Hog

If you want a subject, look to pork!
  Charles Dickens, *Great Expectations*

As the hazy days of autumn slowly replaced the long, hot summers in early Canada, our ancestors faced their annual challenge of preserving enough food to feed their families during the approaching winter. With the coming of the frost and the cold weather, farmers would decide which animals could be kept in the barns until spring and which would be slaughtered for the family table, for bartering with neighbours, or for sale in nearby towns and villages.

Faced with the problems of vast distances to market and a pioneer economy, people were forced to depend on their own resources to survive. They brought with them two basic pieces of information about food preservation: the knowledge that salt — either in a brine or dry — in combination with meat preserved it for long periods of time, and that when moisture was removed from food by sun or air, it too retarded spoiling. If smoke from certain pungent fuels was also added the ultimate result was greatly enhanced in flavour.

The settlers, particularly those of British origin, were very fond of beef but found that in this new country pigs were much easier to raise on their pioneer homesteads, newly carved out of the forests. Cattle could forage for a time in the summer, but eventually their diet had to be supplemented. A pig could easily survive by eating scraps or foraging endlessly in the wild, and a sow could easily raise her piglets with very little help from the owner, thus providing a source of food for months to come. Perhaps for this reason pork was tradition-ally the predominant meat in North America for decades.

Pigs had been domesticated during the Stone Age, and wild pigs may have even crossed the Bering Strait from Russia to disperse through both North and South America, for Hernando Cortes found pigs in Mexico when he arrived in 1519. The first record of domesticated pigs is of the thirteen brought from Spain to Tampa, Florida in 1539 by Hernando de Soto. From this group, it is believed, all North American hogs are descended.

Salting, either in brine or by rubbing with salt, and smoking were the standard methods of treating a butchered hog. Children learned the basic steps in its preservation by watching and helping their families with the slaughtering, salting, and smoking. *The Cook Not Mad* gave basic instruc-tions and also a warning to the uninitiated:

To Salt Pork
Sprinkle salt in the bottom of the barrel, and take care to sprinkle the same plentifully between each layer afterwards. Let the layers be packed very snug by hav-ing the pieces cut of about equal width, say five or six inches, and place edgewise, the rind being towards the barrel. Pork will only take a proper quantity of salt, be

there ever so much in the barrel. The surplus answers for another time. *Caution* — Although the same brine will answer for pickling beef, as that for hams, and the lean parts of pork, yet the two kinds of meat should not be in the brine at the same time. A small piece of beef placed in a barrel where there is pork, would spoil the latter quickly. A beef barrel, likewise, should never be used for pork, no matter how thoroughly scalded or cleansed.

Many settlers who wanted to preserve meat and also improve its flavour by smoking did not have the time or means to build a smokehouse. A reasonable alternative was to hang the meat up the flue of their cooking fireplace, or in a smoke chamber beside the fireplace. Some of these chambers still exist in early Canadian homes. When the meat was hung up the flue, however, there was always the danger of accidents as described by Anne Langton in *A Gentlewoman in Upper Canada*, the story of her life here between 1834 and 1846:

> We had a misfortune this morning. A ham we had put to smoke down the chimney got somewhat over roasted, so the meat slipped out of the skin and came tumbling down upon the fire, all broken to pieces, but we got a little savoury picking out of it.

The Housekeeper's Book, 1837, gives another version of pickling meat and also instructions for its care after pickling and smoking:

To Cure Hams

Let a leg of pork hang for three days, then beat it with
a rolling-pin, and rub into it one ounce of saltpeter,
finely powdered, and mixed with a small quantity of
common salt, then let it lie all night. Make the following pickle: a quart of stale strong beer, half a
pound of bay salt, half a pound of common salt, and
the same of brown sugar, boil this for fifteen or twenty minutes, and then wipe the ham, dry from the salt,
and, with a wooden ladle, pour the pickle, by degrees,
and as hot as possible, over the ham; and as it cools,
rub it well into every part. Rub and turn the ham
every day, for a week, and then hang it, for a fortnight,
in a wood smoke chimney. When you take it down,
sprinkle black pepper over the bone, and into the
holes, to keep it safe from hoppers, and hang up the
ham in a thick paper bag.

For those farmers who built their own smokehouses,
there were a number of things to consider in its construction.
It was imperative that it be sealed and secure against insects,
animals, and rodents that wanted in, and against the smoke
that wanted out. This meant chinking between the logs or
boards with mud, and a stone foundation to discourage rats
and mice from burrowing under the bottom logs or boards to
gain entrance. A dirt floor kept it cool, and a board roof dis-
couraged heat and moisture from gathering.

The ideal timetable for the pioneer farmer was to kill
the hog(s) in early November at the time of the first frost,

coat all sides of the warm meat with plain salt, and leave it to be absorbed for several days. The meat thus cured by this dry method could then be placed on raised racks or shelves in barrels until it was to be smoked. Many settlers used a brine (a barrel of water to which salt had been added until an egg or a raw potato would float on top), in which they immersed the freshly slaughtered meat. The farmer hoped for a cold winter to aid in the preservation process, and if the family needed meat, they would simply cut off a piece, wash it well, parboil it, and then finish cooking by frying or roasting.

This was also the time for sausage to be made. Sausages have a long, honourable history. They were great favourites with the ancient Greeks and Romans — the Greeks called them *oryae*, while the Romans used the term *salsus*, from the Latin word for salted. Emperor Constantine the Great considered them a royal dish, much too fine for common consumption; however, those early sausages would have been much too bland for our taste. In fact, it wasn't until the Middle Ages that cooks began to experiment with various meats, spices, and herbs when making sausages. Many countries developed their own specialties. For example, China contributed a sausage called *lop chong,* made with either pork or liver, steamed with rice, and sliced and served as an *hors d'oeuvre*. Quality could vary tremendously, as many countries developed their own recipes, depending on the proportion of meat to other ingredients. This is probably why sausages became known as "little bags of mystery" during the Victorian era.

To ensure that Canadians were not eating "little bags of mystery," recipes, instructions, and guides were published on the topic. Just one example, *Home Pork Making*, 1910, was described as "a complete guide for the farmer, the country butcher and the suburban dweller, in all that pertains to hog slaughtering, curing, preserving and storing pork product — from scalding vat to kitchen table and dining room." One chapter is devoted to the proper making of sausage and reminds us:

> Like pure lard, sausage is too often a scarce article in the market. Most city butchers mix a good deal of beef with the pork before it is ground, and so have a sausage composed of two sorts of meat, which does not possess that agreeable, sweet, savoury taste peculiar to nice fresh pork ... After sausage is properly ground, add salt, sage, rosemary, and red or black pepper to suit the taste. The rosemary may be omitted, but sage is essential ... If sausage is to be kept in jars, pack it away closely in them, as soon as it is ground and seasoned, and set the jars, securely closed, in a cool room. But it is much better to provide for smoking some of it, to keep through the spring and early summer. When the entrails are ready stuff them full with meat, after which the ends are tied and drawn together, the sausage hung up in the smokehouse for smoking.

There follow recipes for Bologna, Westphalian, Frankfurt, Subian, Italian, Tongue, Black Forest, Liver, Royal Cambridge, Brain, Tomato, and Spanish sausages.

In the spring, about four months after it had been put to cure, the rest of the meat would be washed, dipped in a barrel of boiling water, coated with borax, pepper, and brown sugar, and hung from the rafters in the smokehouse. A slow, smouldering fire was built in a large iron container using hickory, cherry, maple, apple, or oak chips, hickory bark, or corncobs as fuel. Softwood was never used, as the resin was injurious to the meat. The slow fire was kept going for several days until the meat developed a brown crust. It was then sewn into cloth or paper bags to protect it from insects and stored in a cool, dry place. Hopefully, every Canadian family had ensured a supply of meat for the entire year until the fall, when the cycle would begin again.

Everyone in a pioneer community understood this cycle and the basic steps needed for success. As a result, terms like "pork barrel legislation" came to mean local favours designed to help a region of the country, while "living high on the hog" meant eating well while others suffered.

The refrigerated railway cars that were developed in 1877 by Gustavus Swift, whose name is still associated with the meat packing industry, brought about a slow revolution in the need to treat large quantities of meat at home. In addition, beef began to compete favourably with the price of pork, and many farmers chose to belong to the local Beef Ring, thus making the revolution complete. Urban dwellers found that they could now purchase the meat of their choice, at a price they could afford, and many a smokehouse fell into disrepair, or was used as a storage shed.

Canadian cookery books of both the past and the present abound with sausage recipes. Here are two old favourites:

Sausage Rolls

Make a rich pie paste, roll out thin and cut, with a large cookie cutter or a canister lid, large discs of the paste. Take a small cooked sausage, and placing it on the edge of the circle of paste, roll it up and pinch the ends together. Bake in a quick oven and serve hot or cold.

Sausage with Cabbage

Put some pieces of fat and lean pork through the sausage mill; add a finely chopped onion, pepper, salt and a dash of mace. Cut a large, sound head of cabbage in two, scoop out the heart of both halves and fill with sausage meat; tie up the head securely with stout twine, put into salted water sufficient to cover the cabbage and boil 1 1/2 hours. Drain thoroughly and save the liquid, which should not exceed one cupful in all. Brown a tablespoonful of butter over a hot fire, stir in a teaspoon of browned flour and add the liquid; pour over cabbage and serve hot.

The annual slaughter, salting, and smoking of meat is one aspect of pioneer life that I suspect passed into memory on some Canadian farms with a sigh of relief. However, many cultural groups across Canada still carry out the annual tasks with pride and pleasure and enjoy the unique products on their table all year long.

Celebrating Cranberries

The Indians and English use them much, boyling them with Sugar for Sauce to eat with their Meat, and it is a delicious sauce.
John Josselyn, while visiting New England in 1663

For many Canadians, Christmas represents the most delicious of all our holidays and holy days. In many homes, traditional family recipes will be used to prepare the sumptuous feast to be enjoyed by family and friends. As part of this command performance, cranberry sauce or cranberry chutney will be right there beside the turkey, goose, or other fowl that is a part of the groaning board. This humble little dish, made from those ruby red berries, has a long and distinguished history.

The First Nations recognized both the culinary and medicinal properties of the high bush cranberry and its smaller cousins, found in the bogs and marshy areas, long before the arrival of the first newcomers to North America. The native peoples enjoyed them both raw and cooked, sometimes sweetened with maple syrup or maple sugar. The bark of the high bush cranberry was used originally to prepare sedatives; however, after the arrival of Europeans and the introduction of a host of new diseases, it was used to treat mumps, among other things. Legend tells us that the First

Nations introduced cranberries to the Pilgrims at the well-known Thanksgiving in 1621, and they may well have been part of that feast. We Canadians should be aware, however, that that was not the *first* Thanksgiving in North America, for it had been celebrated for many years in various locations in what is today Atlantic Canada. The new arrivals adapted the "bog berries" or "crane berries," as they often called them, to their own recipes and medicines. They recognized their properties as a diuretic and as an aid in treating urinary infections, attributes that have been proven by modern medical science.

The French, who called them *canneberge*, served them to their sailors to ward off scurvy in the navy, and the Germans, who called them mooseberries, cowberries, and foxberries, used them whole and cooked with wild game as sauces and spreads.

The United Empire Loyalists who arrived in what is now Nova Scotia were delighted to find this familiar berry already growing there, and in 1860 cultivation of cranberries began. In those early days harvesters going out into the bogs would have worn large hats, heavy canvas aprons, and knee patches for protection and would have bound their hands or worn heavy gloves. They would then have scooped up the red harvest with a wooden scoop and dropped it into a container. For years the traditional uses for cranberries, in addition to their healing properties, were in sauces, chutneys, puddings, and pies. For over a century, the unchanging recipe for cranberry sauce has served Canadians at our Thanksgiving, Christmas, and other festive tables:

Cranberry Sauce
1 cup water
1 cup granulated sugar
12 ounces fresh cranberries

In a medium-sized saucepan, combine water and sugar and bring to boil. Add cranberries and return to a boil and continue to boil gently, stirring occasionally for about 10 minutes. Cover and cool at room temperature. Refrigerate until ready to serve.

In the nineteenth and early twentieth centuries, a favourite recipe right across Canada was one for mock cherry pie, using cranberries as a substitute for the often elusive, and more expensive, cherries:

Mock Cherry Pie
3 1/2 cups cranberries (cut in halves)
1 1/2 cup sugar
1 teaspoon vanilla
1 tablespoon flour, dissolved in 1/2 cup water
1 egg

Mix well and bake between two crusts of your favourite pastry.

Every Canadian housewife would have known how to prepare cranberry tea as a preventative or a restorative. This recipe appeared in *Health in the Household*, written by Susanna W. Dodds, A.M., M.D., in 1888:

Cranberry Tea
Take ripe cranberries, perfectly sound, mash thoroughly, and pour boiling water over them; let the mixture stand a few minutes, or till cold; then strain off the water, and sweeten to taste.

Cranberries were one of the easiest of fruits to keep over the winter, contrary to many others. *The Farmer's and Housekeeper's Cyclopaedia* tells us:

To Keep Cranberries all Winter — Put them in a cool room, where there is no danger of freezing, and either spread out on a cloth, so as to give each berry light and air; or, which is a sure way, put them in a barrel under water.

The twentieth century has brought a revolution to the cultivation and consumption of cranberries. Not only Canadians but also markets around the world are looking for cranberries at every season of the year, not just at Thanksgiving and Christmas. We find them in juice, cereal, yogurt, ice cream, syrup, relish, conserve, catsup, compote, punch, cookies, cakes, muffins, parfaits, and a host of other recipes. We not only enjoy their tart flavour, but we also bask in the knowledge that they are good for us as they contain iodine, calcium, and vitamins A and C. They are also good for our economy, as cranberries are one of the few commercially harvested fruits native to North America. British Columbia, Nova Scotia, Quebec, and Ontario are not only producers but also celebrate their production with festivals while they are harvested in the late summer and the early fall.

Cranberries can be added to many of our favourite recipes with sparkling results, both in colour and flavour. Cranberries can, and do, appear in every course that we might serve at our tables, and as snacks and beverages. Here are some suggestions:

Cranberry Apple Soup
1 tablespoon butter
1/2 cup fresh cranberries, rinsed in cold water and picked over
2 cups apples, peeled and coarsely chopped
2 cups chicken stock
1 1/2 teaspoons honey
1 cup milk

Melt the butter in a heavy saucepan. Add the apple and cranberries and cook, covered, over low heat for about ten minutes. Put in a blender or food processor and blend until smooth. Strain through a sieve and return to the saucepan, add the chicken stock, honey, and milk. Heat, but do not boil. Serve hot or cold. Makes four servings.

Chutney, a condiment that originated in India, is very popular in Canada at the present time. This recipe for cranberry chutney evolved in my own kitchen one day when I wanted to make chutney and realized I didn't have the ingredients for any of my recipes in the house, and I did not want to go shopping. I have found that this chutney is not only a fine companion for turkey and other fowl, but also for pork, beef, ham, and just about anything else you want to pair it with.

Dorothy's Cranberry Chutney
1 1/2 cups cider vinegar
2 1/2 cups firmly packed brown sugar
1/2 teaspoon ground ginger
1/4 teaspoon ground cloves
1/2 teaspoon cinnamon
1 lemon, rind grated, pith discarded, fruit cut into sections
1 orange, rind grated, pith discarded, fruit cut into sections
2 apples, peeled and coarsely chopped
8 cups cranberries, picked over and washed
1 cup golden raisins
1 cup chopped dried apricots
1 cup chopped walnuts (optional)

In a large saucepan combine the vinegar, sugar, ginger, cloves, cinnamon, and 1 1/2 cups of water and bring to a boil, stirring until the sugar is dissolved.

Add lemon and orange rind, lemon and orange sections, and the apples; simmer, stirring occasionally, for 10 minutes. Add half the cranberries and all the raisins and apricots and simmer, stirring occasionally, for 30 minutes or until it thickens. Add the remaining cranberries and simmer for about 15 minutes. Finally add the walnuts and simmer for 15 minutes, stirring often. Spoon the hot chutney into sterilized jars, tapping to eliminate any air bubbles. Seal with the lids and store in a cool, dark place. Makes about 10 cups and will keep in the refrigerator for several months.

The spirit of celebration is captured in a colourful cranberry pudding with its bright, juicy, red flashes of colour. You can make it even more colourful by flaming your pudding when it is time to bring it to the table!

Cranberry Pudding
6 tablespoons butter
3/4 cup sugar
2 eggs
2 1/4 cups sifted all-purpose flour
2 1/2 teaspoons baking powder
1/4 teaspoon salt
1/2 cup milk
2 cups cranberries

In a large mixing bowl, cream the butter and sugar, add the eggs, and beat well. Sift the flour, baking powder, and salt together and add to the creamed mixture alternately with the milk. Stir in the cranberries. Grease a mould or pudding dish and pour in the mixture. Cover with a pudding cloth or foil. Secure with string. Place in a large saucepan or steamer on a rack and half fill with water. Bring water to boil and cover. Steam for 2 hours. Lift out and let stand for 15 minutes, turn upside down, and unmould. It can be served at once with sauce, stored in the refrigerator for several days, or cooled, wrapped, and frozen to use later.

You may want to try this Surprise sauce instead of your traditional one as it is particularly well suited to cranberry pudding.

Surprise Sauce
1 cup butter
1 1/2 cups sugar
1 cup commercial egg nog
1 tablespoon rum or rum flavouring

Combine the butter, sugar, and eggnog in a saucepan and simmer until heated through, stirring occasionally. Stir in rum or rum flavouring and remove from heat. Makes about 3 cups of sauce.

Another colourful and easy dessert can be made by simply baking cranberries in the following way:

Candied Cranberries

Spread about 1 pound of freshly washed cranberries on a greased baking pan, sprinkle with 2 1/2 cups sugar, and let stand for about 1 hour. Cover with foil and bake at 350°F for about 45 minutes, stirring occasionally. Remove from oven and cool. Spoon into dessert dishes (glass if possible), chill, and serve with whipped cream.

Experiment with cranberries — add a few to your favourite salad, muffins, bread, or pie recipe. Join the growing number of Canadian cooks and chefs who are finding that this versatile little berry is indeed a gift for all seasons, and keep on tossing it into those recipes!

Festive Fowl and Forcemeat

Poultry is for cookery what canvas is for painting, and the cap of Fortunatus for the charlatans. It is served to us boiled, roast, hot or cold, whole or in portions, with or without sauce, and always with equal success.
Jean-Anthelme Brillat-Savarin

Canadians, whether First Nations or newcomers, have been celebrating with hearty meals shared with family, friends, and neighbours for centuries. Whether a religious, seasonal, or personal celebration, fowl has usually been an important addition to the festive table. One of the earliest descriptions of a Canadian Christmas comes from the journal of Thomas Gorst in 1670. The ships *Wivenhoe* and *Prince Rupert* were wintering at Charles Fort on James Bay, and Governor Charles Bayley, Sieur des Grosseillers, Pierre Esprit Radisson, and Captain Gillam were the guests:

> 25 being Christmas, wee made merry remembering our Friends in England, having for Liquor Brandy and strong beer and for Food plenty of Partridges and Venson besides what ye shipps provisions afforded.

Many legends abound about the tradition of serving fowl at celebrations, including the popularity of roast goose

235

as the principal dish. *Cassells Dictionary of Cookery; Containing about Nine Thousand Recipes,* 1877 tells us:

> It is said that Queen Elizabeth was the originator of the Michaelmas goose. She had one on the table before her, when the news arrived of the defeat of the Spanish Armada, and she commanded the same dish to be served every succeeding Michaelmas.

Through the years Canadians have shown a preference for turkey to grace their tables at Christmas. It was Isabella Beeton, writing in *The Book of Household Management,* 1861, who set the record straight about the origins and popularity of the turkey:

> The turkey, for which fine bird we are indebted to America, is certainly one of the most glorious presents made by the New World to the Old. Some, indeed, assert that this bird was known to the ancients, and that it was served at the wedding feast of Charlemagne. This opinion, however, has been controverted by first-rate authorities, who declare that the French name of the bird, *dindon,* proves its origin; that the form of the bird is altogether foreign, and that it is found in America alone in a wild state. There is but little doubt, from the information which has been gained at considerable trouble, that it appeared generally, in Europe about the end of the 17th

century; that it was first imported into France by Jesuits, who had been sent out as missionaries to the West; and that from France it spread over Europe. To this day, in many localities in France, a turkey is called a *jesuit*.

On the farms of N. America, where turkeys are very common, they are raised either from eggs which have been found, or from young ones caught in the woods; they thus preserve almost entirely their original plumage. The turkey only became gradually acclimated, both on the continent and in England in the middle of the 18th century, scarcely 10 out of 20 young turkeys lived; now generally speaking, 15 out of the same number arrive at maturity.

Canadians who kept diaries in the nineteenth century confirm the continuing popularity of turkey. In 1800, Joseph Willcocks, a resident of York (Toronto), described Christmas Day in his diary: "Went to Church. Weekes dined with us. We had for dinner, soup, roast beef, boiled Pork, Turkey, Plumb Pudding and minced pies." In Penetanguishene, Upper Canada (Ontario), in 1846, Sarah and Ellen Hallen, daughters of the curate of St. James on the Lines, confirm the continuing tradition: "We all went to church, roads not good, this church beautifully decorated and for dinner we had an immense turkey, so glad we were all together."

As wave after wave of immigrants arrived in North America, they brought with them a love of every kind of poultry and game, and as a result Canadian cookery books contained recipes for every possible method of preparing turkeys, chickens, goslings and geese, ducks, squab, ruffed grouse, prairie chickens, partridge, quail, and pigeons. These recipes could be used for the holiday bird or, of course, for the everyday round of meal preparation.

In, fact, it was the early Canadian settlers' enjoyment of the wild passenger pigeon on their dinner tables that led to its extinction. These migratory pigeons appeared over the eastern provinces in August and blackened the sky with their vast numbers, making an easy target for hunters using both guns and nets. By 1914 they had vanished.

Once the bird is chosen many of us will prepare a succulent mixture to fill the cavity in the bird. This mixture has been known as forcemeat, stuffing, and dressing. Forcemeat is the oldest term, coming from the French word *farcir*, to stuff or to force. In 1538 the word "stuffing" appeared for the first time, and the two words were then often used interchangeably. During the Victorian period, "dressing" became a more acceptable term in polite society.

Whatever the name, the filling often equals or surpasses in flavour whatever is being filled, and it can take many forms: crumbs of white, brown, or corn bread combined with seasonings, fat, and liquids; chopped and/or cooked vegetables such as onions, potatoes, and celery; mushrooms; meats such as bacon, sausage, cold beef, pork, or lamb; seafood; or rice, fruit, and nuts. All can be used either singly or in combination with one another.

Recipes for forcemeats and stuffings go back several centuries; they began to appear in Great Britain in the

1400s, with the yolks of hard-boiled eggs as the basic ingredient, rather than the bread crumbs that we expect today. This fifteenth-century recipe is typical:

> *To Stuff a Chicken*
> 5 or 6 hard-boiled egg yolks
> 1/2 cup parsley, blanched and finely chopped
> 1/4 cup butter
> 1/8 teaspoon fresh ginger, finely chopped
> 1/4 teaspoon pepper
> 1/4 teaspoon salt
> 1/8 teaspoon saffron

As you select and prepare your festive fowl, you should be prepared to do a little extra work to ensure a tasty centerpiece for your meal. Unless you raise your own, know someone who does, or can shop at a farmer's market, you are probably buying a bird that has been raised in a controlled environment, and likely it will require seasoning to enhance the flavour lost to modern methods of breeding and raising. Once you have selected the bird, and thoroughly washed it both inside and out with salted water, any remaining feathers should be removed. Dry the bird thoroughly, and prepare to add some extra flavour: this should go inside the bird in the form of some salt and pepper, some whole onions, a liberal rub with parsley butter, or a good stuffing. Most birds (particularly chicken) will benefit from a liberal massage with cooking oil to seal the skin and give a uniform sheen when it comes from the oven.

Nineteenth- and twentieth-century cookery books provide us with some simple recipes for stuffing a goose to offset the excessive fat that is found in some of them. Our traditions have changed very little over the years, for we find virtually the same recipe in *The New Galt Cook Book*, published in Toronto in 1898, and the classic *Out of Nova Scotia Kitchens*, by Marie Nightingale in 1971, for:

Potato Stuffing
Take two-thirds bread, one-third boiled potatoes grated, butter size of an egg, pepper, salt, one egg and a little ground sage, mix thoroughly.

The success of your Christmas dinner will not only depend upon the flavour of your fowl but also, to some degree, on the condiments that you serve with it. Many of these can be purchased already prepared; however, you may want to make your own well in advance of The Day. Store them in a cool place, and bring them forward with a flourish to grace the table and add an extra dimension to the chosen bird.

Bread Sauce
Many Canadian families have their own traditional recipe for this favourite. Here is a modern version of an old English recipe.

Boil 1/4 pint milk with a finely chopped onion and 2 or 3 whole cloves for about 5 or 6 minutes. Remove the cloves and add about 1 cup of fresh white breadcrumbs. Simmer for five minutes, and then stir in 1/2 ounce butter, 1/4 pint cereal cream, and a sprinkle of pepper, salt, and nutmeg. Serve with turkey.

Apple Sauce

Apple sauce makes a fine companion to pork at any time of the year, and a particularly fine companion to goose at Christmas.

Peel, quarter, and core six apples and put into a saucepan with a small amount of water and 3 whole cloves. Cook on low heat for ten minutes with the lid on the pan. Add 2 tablespoons of red currant jelly and stir well. Put through a sieve, put back in the saucepan, and add a pinch of salt. Serve warm or cold.

A Canadian Christmas, like so many other celebrations, is a mixture of traditions — those of our ancestors and those we have developed on our own. Make this Christmas in your home a happy blending of your traditions, both old and new.

The Proof Is in the Pudding

Flour of England, fruit of Spain, Met together in a shower of rain,
Put in a bag, tied round with a string
If you'll tell me this riddle I'll give you a ring.
   Nineteenth-century riddle

Most Canadians would not be surprised to learn that the answer to this nineteenth-century riddle is the plum pudding. When we mention the word pudding, we most often envision that round, brown, fruit-filled, steamed, boiled, or baked Victorian dessert, covered with sauce and served during the Christmas season. In reality, not only has the plum pudding much earlier origins, but puddings in one form or another have been with us since Roman times. The Romans stuffed their pudding mixtures into animal intestines and then dropped them into the same boiling cauldron as the meat, and when all was ready they ate the pudding in place of bread.

Puddings have continued to be a combination of several ingredients used to stretch a meal, and because they could be made either savoury or sweet, they could be part of the main course, the dessert, or even comprise a whole meal. What to cook the pudding in was always a dilemma — in addition to intestines, hollowed-out vegetables such as potatoes, carrots, and turnips were tried. It was a great innovation when in the seventeenth century the pudding cloth was first used and proven to be an appropriate container for this increasingly popular dish. Puddings could be made of any combination of flour or stale flour products such as bread or biscuits mixed with chopped vegetables, fruits, seasonings, and fat. As puddings spread across Europe, every cultural group changed them to suit their needs and culinary traditions.

It was probably the conquering Danes who introduced the plum pudding to Great Britain in 1013, but in a form unrecognizable to modern Canadians. It began as a broth, developed into a thickened pottage or porridge, and finally, by the eighteenth century, when batter puddings were becoming popular and the pudding cloth was available, took on the form and shape we recognize today. The original recipes called for minced meat (as did many pudding recipes). Through the years, however, the minced meat has usually been replaced by additional fruit.

The British took puddings, whether savoury or sweet, hot or cold, to their hearts and developed hundreds of recipes for them. They ranged from the simple to the elegant, and their names were very descriptive of exactly what the puddings would contain or how they would taste. These three are just a sample:

Bread and Butter Pudding
Get a penny loaf, and cut it into thin slices of bread and butter as you do for tea. Butter your dish as you

cut them. Lay slices all over the dish, then strew a few currants clean washed and picked, then a row of bread and butter, then a few currants, and so on until all your bread and butter is in. Then take a pint of milk, beat up four eggs, a little salt, half a nutmeg grated; mix all together with sugar to your taste. Pour this over the bread and bake it for half an hour. You may put in two spoonfuls of rose water.

The Art of Cookery made Plain and Easy, Mrs. Hannah Glasse, 1747

Another and perhaps more interesting name for this pudding was the Poor Knights of Windsor, which could be made as above or with the bread soaked in sherry then dipped in beaten egg yolks and fried. A sauce of sherry, sugar, and butter was served over the pudding. Obviously, the knights eating this version were not quite so poor!

A Spoonful Pudding

Take a spoonful of flour, a spoonful of cream, or milk, an egg, a little nutmeg, ginger, and salt. Mix all together and boil it in a little wooden dish half an hour. If you think proper you may add a few currants.

The Housekeeper's Instructor, William Augustus Henderson, 1790

Plum Pudding

To three ounces of flour, and the same weight of fine lightly grated breadcrumbs, add six of beef kidney-suet chopped small, six of raisins weighed after they are stoned, six of well cleaned currants, four ounces of minced apples, five of sugar, two of candied orange-rind, half a teaspoonful of nutmeg mixed with powdered mace, a very little salt, a small glass of brandy, and three whole eggs. Mix and beat these ingredients well together, tie them tightly in a thickly floured cloth, and boil them for three hours and a half. We can recommend this as a remarkably light small rich pudding. It may be served with German wine or punch sauce.

The Dinner Question, Tabitha Tickletooth, 1860

Symbols to foretell the future were often baked into cakes and puddings. In 1896, Mrs. Humphrey tells us in her *Cookery Up-to-Date*:

the pudding served on Christmas Day should contain a silver thimble, a gold or silver ring, a large Spanish nut, a large bone button. Whoever gets the money will be lucky throughout the approaching year. The thimble and button portend celibacy during the same period. The nut means wealth.

The settlers arriving in British North America in the late eighteenth and early nineteenth centuries brought their love of puddings with them. To their surprise, they found that the First Nations had long been making a traditional pudding-like dish with cornmeal as a basic ingredient. It eventually became known by many names, including Indian Pudding, Canadian Pudding, and Grandmother's Pudding. This recipe, and the maple syrup that is often served with it, has continued to be a popular dessert on many tables across Canada.

Indian Corn Flour Pudding
2 ounces Indian corn flour
1/2 pint milk
3/4 pint boiling milk
1 egg
sweetening and flavouring to taste

This must not be confounded with corn flour sold in packets, which in some cases is the starch of Indian corn or maize, deprived of much of its nutritive value by the process it undergoes to render it white and smooth. Indian corn flour is the finely-ground flour of maize. Properly prepared, it furnishes a wholesome, digestible and nutritious food. Like oatmeal, it requires to be thoroughly well boiled. Vanilla is the most suitable flavouring for this pudding, but any other may be used. Mix the corn flour smooth in the cold milk and then stir in the boiling milk. Sweeten and flavour. Put into a clean stewpan and stir over the fire until it becomes thick; beat in the egg, put the pudding in a buttered tart dish and bake very slowly for three-quarters of an hour.

The Proof Is in the Pudding

The above recipe is from *The Dominion Cook Book*, published in 1899 and compiled by Anne Clark. This book contains over seventy-five recipes for puddings and a multitude of sauces to serve on them, but it still doesn't match *The Book of Household Management*, by Isabella Beeton, 1861, containing over two hundred pudding recipes!

The heyday for the pudding continued well into the twentieth century for Canadians, since puddings were versatile, cheap, easily and quickly made, and designed to fill an empty stomach. To support this interest and demand a variety of pudding moulds and basins were designed. The classic English pudding basin is white earthenware and capable of withstanding the heat of steaming for several hours. Copper and tin moulds were also popular, particularly in the nineteenth and early twentieth centuries, as some of them had a fitted lid that could be used for steamed puddings.

In the twentieth century we were seduced by instant foods. Prime among them have been the custards, jellies, and other easy-to-prepare desserts that masquerade as puddings. If you would like to return to one of the favourite foods of our ancestors, whether they be First Nations or newcomers, take out your mixing bowl and spoon and prepare one of the following time-honoured recipes.

The most popular pudding coast to coast across Canada is one that has many names: Hard Times Pudding, My Favourite Pudding, Caramel Pudding, Conservative Pudding with Liberal Sauce, Liberal Pudding with Conservative Sauce, and more. It was, and still is, perfect for every occasion.

My Favourite Pudding
1 cup flour
1/2 cup brown sugar
2 teaspoons baking powder
pinch salt
1 cup raisins or currants (well washed and dried)
1/2 cup milk
2 tablespoons butter

Sauce:
1 cup brown sugar
1 tablespoon butter
2 cups boiling water

Butter an 8-inch casserole or baking dish, mix the batter well and put in the casserole. Pour sauce over batter slowly and place in a 350°F oven and bake for about 30 minutes. As it bakes, batter will rise to the top and the sauce will go to the bottom of the dish. Makes 6 to 8 servings and is best served warm.

For those early birds who are already thinking ahead to the holiday season, here is a Christmas pudding recipe that was first made in the family of my maternal grandmother, Georgina Lyon Gibson. Georgina was born in Aberdeen, Scotland in 1853 and kept a hand-written booklet of recipes. My family has memorized many of them, and we continue to use them at all seasons of the year. It is interesting to see how often this recipe (or a close approximation) appears across Canada in such fine collections as *From Saskatchewan Homemakers' Kitchens*, 1955.

Carrot Pudding
1 teaspoon baking soda
1/4 cup milk or 1 egg
1 cup grated potato
1 cup grated carrot
1 1/2 cups flour
1 1/2 cups suet
1 cup chopped muscat raisins
1 cup currants
1 cup sugar
1 teaspoon salt
1 teaspoon cinnamon
1 teaspoon nutmeg
1/4 teaspoon ground cloves

Dissolve the soda in the milk or beaten egg. Mix all ingredients well, and steam in a covered bowl for 3 hours. Keep in a cold, dry place until needed. This pudding freezes well. When ready to use, steam for 15 to 20 minutes and serve with sauce, whipped cream or your favourite topping.

"Blessed be he that invented pudding," said Mission de Valberg, a nineteenth-century visitor to England. "It is a manna that hits the palates of all sorts of people; a manna better than that of the wilderness, because the people are never weary of it … to come in pudding time is as much to say, to come in the most lucky moment in the world."

When the days begin to lengthen and you prepare for another Canadian winter, pudding time has arrived. Explore these lucky moments in your kitchen.